The Invention of Green Colonialism

The Invention of Green Colonialism

GUILLAUME BLANC

Translated by Helen Morrison

polity

Originally published in French as *L'invention du colonialisme vert. Pour en finir avec le mythe d'Éden africain*. Préface de François-Xavier Fauvelle © Flammarion, Paris, 2020

This English edition © Polity Press, 2022

1892 maps of Ethiopia: 'Carta dimostrativa dell' Etiopia'. Credit: Library of Congress, Geography and Map Division.

Polity Press
65 Bridge Street
Cambridge CB2 1UR, UK

Polity Press
101 Station Landing
Suite 300
Medford, MA 02155, USA

ISBN-13: 978-1-5095-5088-3
ISBN-13: 978-1-5095-5089-0 (paperback)

A catalogue record for this book is available from the British Library.

Typeset in 11 on 14pt Warnock Pro
by Cheshire Typesetting Ltd, Cuddington, Cheshire
Printed and bound in Great Britain by CPI Group (UK) Ltd, Croydon

The publisher has used its best endeavours to ensure that the URLs for external websites referred to in this book are correct and active at the time of going to press. However, the publisher has no responsibility for the websites and can make no guarantee that a site will remain live or that the content is or will remain appropriate.

Every effort has been made to trace all copyright holders, but if any have been overlooked the publisher will be pleased to include any necessary credits in any subsequent reprint or edition.

For further information on Polity, visit our website:
politybooks.com

Contents

Preface to the English Edition
History as a Starting Point

*T*he *Invention of Green Colonialism.* By virtue of its title,
as soon as it was published, this book was associated
with postcolonial studies, even with 'decolonial' thinking. These fields of study have of course influenced my work,
but what I wanted first and foremost was to write a book focusing on environmental history. With this discipline, 'we can
create a more usable past, one more relevant to the everyday
lives of people today', as Ted Steinberg puts it. And to do that,
the American historian tells us, we need to re-establish 'the
way power operates through and across landscape'.[1]

Still in North America, this time in Canada, Stéphane
Castonguay explains how we can achieve this. There is no
point in trying to distinguish between the natural and the cultural, given that in the world around us, everything is hybrid.
However, Castonguay explains, the environmental historian
can decipher the mechanisms which result in a landscape
ending up being defined in one place as 'natural' and in another
as 'cultural'. And for that to be achieved, nature needs to be
regarded as a battleground: the institutional battle over how a
territory is controlled, the cultural battle to establish an image
of the environment in the public domain and the material

battle over the exploitation of a resource.[2] In this book, these
three dimensions of social relationships with nature are a constant presence.

Let us begin with the institutional aspect. For many environmental historians, confining nature within a park represents
a double act of appropriation and of disappropriation. This
is the case everywhere and perhaps particularly in Africa.
Under colonial rule, the colonists first set about creating
hunting reserves as a way of demonstrating their capacity to
dominate nature and space.[3] Next it was the turn of European
administrations to use the national parks as a means to better
control, manage and suppress populations.[4] Then, once the
postcolonial period had begun, the international conservation institutions continued to impose coercive models for the
protection of nature, models which involved displacing local
people, restricting right of access to resources and criminalizing use of the land.[5] The majority of those African states called
upon to put these programmes in place took advantage of the
situation to impose tighter controls over their citizens.[6] And
the latter therefore found themselves seeking out any available
gaps which would enable them to get round the conservation
rules, and even to use them to exercise political advantage
over their neighbours and their communities.[7] Put differently,
for all the actors involved in the institutionalization of the
environment, protecting nature always involves the exercise
of power.

However, if it is to be effective, this power to define the
'good' and 'bad' use of nature needs to be underpinned by a
certain number of specific perceptions – of the 'good' images
of nature, to put it briefly. Environmental historians have long
clashed over this issue, wondering whether the way we *think
about* nature might or might not affect the way we *conserve*
it. William Cronon, a major theoretician of the American
wilderness, made a positive contribution to this debate by
demonstrating that 'pristine' nature was never a reality but,

primarily, 'the reflection of our own unexamined longings and desires'.[8] And no matter how elitist they are, 'ideas do matter', as Cronon reminds us.[9] Here too, the argument is particularly relevant to contemporary African societies. By linking the field of perceptions of nature with that of political action, many historians have shown the determining nature of the European and, later, western vision of Africa. A steadily increasing media coverage in the form of travel journals, novels, guidebooks, wildlife documentaries or animated films has, over the course of more than a century, portrayed Africa as a supremely natural landscape, sadly damaged by its inhabitants. Yet perceiving African ecologies as 'wild things'[10] implies wanting to experience them as such and, consequently, needing to protect them as such. This is why it is crucial always to link conservation norms to the emotions and affects which govern their definition. If we wish to understand why conservationists are still determined to make the African national parks wild spaces, we need to ask how it was that they came to believe that 'good' African nature is always uninhabited.

Finding an answer to this question also means considering the material dimension underlying social relationships with nature. The British historian Richard Grove was the first person to throw light on the links between ecologism and capitalism. The more Europeans cultivated, exploited and damaged the soil and the wildlife of the tropics, the more determined they were to protect the environment from this destruction. Except that, in order to do so, they restricted the rights of 'local indigenous people', accused of destroying nature and therefore needing to be removed.[11] And since that time, this dual concept of predation/protection has continued to shape global policies for nature in Africa. The imperatives of the capitalist economy cause ever more damage, ecological demands result in the creation of a growing number of protected zones, and farmers and shepherds are once again seen as those largely responsible for the massive deterioration of the environment.[12]

Many environmental historians have turned their attention to this anti-rural ethic. Yet, very often, one question remains unresolved: what is it that these famous 'indigenous people', constantly singled out, but then ignored, by the conservationists, actually do? For the majority of them, as Ramachandra Guha and Madhav Gadgil demonstrated in India as early as 1992, ecologism only serves to exacerbate their poverty.[13] That said, since farmers and shepherds continue to exploit the land, they also fall into the category of 'environmental banditry', as Karl Jacoby points out with reference to the United States.[14] And since the 1980s, in Africa, in Asia or in Latin America, given that those who live in the natural world are also trying to earn a living from the new community conservation, this can result in confrontations, divisions and conflicts between them. It is one of the main consequences of 'the tyranny' of participation in that once nature becomes monetized, there will inevitably be both losers and winners.[15]

Consequently, inside the national parks, everyone finds themselves caught up in the struggle to control, represent and exploit nature. This principle lies at the heart of environmental history, and is central to this book. However, the book also draws on at least three other fields of study.

In the first place, postcolonial studies allow us to simultaneously observe global conservation and the form it takes locally: that is to say, the system and the individuals, from the top to the bottom. The work of Edward Said[16] helps us, for example, to have a better understanding of the injustice of global policies which, in Africa, involve criminalizing those who live off and in the natural world. What kind of discourse could have succeeded in convincing western conservationists of the radical otherness of African peasants? What discursive practices could ever have justified this approach to the Other ('the African'), an attitude which would, moreover, be morally unacceptable in western societies? As for this 'Other', the difficulty lies in being able to identify him or her, not just as a passive subject, but as a fully participating actor. The work of Gayatri Chakravorty Spivak sets us on the right track here. By formulating the famous question 'Can the subaltern speak?' the literary theorist urges us to restore a voice to those whom power has silenced. It is a process which requires work on a personal level – trying to see the world through the eyes of others – as well as on a historical one – tracking down, in the sources produced by the dominant, the actions of the dominated.[17] In this book, by mixing archives and real-life stories, I have therefore tried always to keep in mind the fact that nature was shaped just as much by those at the top as by those at the bottom, each having a role to play in the invention of green colonialism.

Because they are produced by authors who fluctuate between a scholarly position and a militant stance, these postcolonial theories can sometimes end up being as useful as they are misleading. So, for example, orientalism as defined by Said can easily edge us towards occidentalism. Just as there is no *single* Africa but instead many African societies, we cannot refer to a *single* western conservation system: there are the international institutions, who negotiate their norms with the African states responsible for applying them. As for the famous 'subaltern' whom so many postcolonial theorists seek to defend, there too the trap of essentialism is never far away. It is an indisputable fact that, in the eyes of the experts and the leaders who judge and govern them, the sub-Saharan African peasants are all too often only a 'third something', this '*tertium quid*' defined by W.E.B. Du Bois to describe the condition of black people in America in the early twentieth century, and recently updated by Paul Gilroy to describe the victims of a 'postcolonial melancholia'.[18] Nevertheless, however much they are dominated, the farmers and shepherds of the African natural parks know how to deal with power, often refusing to accept it and finding a way around it, sometimes appropriating it themselves and imposing it on their neighbours.

The main difficulty of this book was therefore to study both the system and the individual, without ever losing sight of the complexity of social life generated by the global government of African nature. This is why two methodological safeguards have guided the story set out in these pages.

The first of these comes from science studies. As Bruno Latour explains, ever since the end of the 1980s, scientific knowledge has been a social construction.[19] Thus, throughout the book, I have tried to envisage conservation experts as 'centres of calculation', as intermediaries who link together the observations made by the personnel of African parks, the data compiled by the international institutions based in the West and the norms produced, in due course, by the national administrations in power. This approach enabled me to define nature as an object enforced and negotiated on a daily basis, constructed and reconstructed at ground level.

This 'bottom-up' approach owes much, finally, to the field of African studies. In the furrow traced by historians such as Frederick Cooper, I have resolutely abandoned all neo-colonial theories and instead focused on dynamics which are specifically African.[20] During the 1960s, the archives reveal ongoing encounters between the colonial administrators subsequently converted into international experts, auxiliaries of colonization now transformed into national leaders, and peasants inured to a regime of submission and resistance. And in postcolonial Africa today, the same type of interactions are still taking place. It is precisely these global African encounters that explain why green colonialism still exerts its influence on the present.

Acknowledgements

Writing history is a collective adventure and this book owes much to many people. My research in Ethiopia could not have taken place without the financial support of the ANR (CE27) PANSER. My thanks also to all the staff at the Ethiopian Wildlife Conservation Authority and at the French Centre for Ethiopian Studies (CFEE) in Addis Ababa. Without the warm welcome and the ongoing help of Fanuel Kebede, Getnet Ygzaw, Kumara Wakijira, Marie Bridonneau and Kidanemaryam Woldegyorgis, I would not have been able to carry out my research.

François-Xavier Fauvelle is a key figure in the conception of this book. I am extremely grateful to him for encouraging me to write it. I would also like to thank Pauline Miel, my editor at Flammarion, France, for her constant support and her unfailing enthusiasm, thoroughness and kindness. Last but not least, without the editorial team of Polity, this book would have remained accessible only for French readers. I am grateful for the opportunity to have worked with John Thompson and Elise Heslinga, and for the enthusiastic rigour of my translator, Helen Morrison.

Thanks also to my colleagues from the history department

in Rennes 2, and in particular to Karim Ghorbal, who was always ready to listen and to advise, in spite of the increasingly demanding conditions of day-to-day university work.

I also owe a great deal to the many people who shared my journey and to the colleagues and friends who encouraged me to draw attention to this little-known, but dramatic, aspect of African history. Thanks to David Annequin, Fiora Badiou, Amélie Chekroun, Romain Favreau, Thomas Guindeuil, Bertrand Hirsch, Julien Horon, Mehdi Labzaé, Victor Magnani, Grégory Quenet, Alexis Roy, Thibaud Trochu and Bérénice Velez. Thank you, above all, for these same reasons and for so many others, to my first reader, Clara Delboé.

Finally, this book should be signed by all the inhabitants of the Simien Mountains in Ethiopia. It is of course only a very small gesture. I simply hope that it will play its part in ensuring that the world hears the story of these women and these men sacrificed in the name of a world heritage in which they have no place, and of a worldwide ecological catastrophe in which they play no part.

Introduction

This story begins with a dream. The dream of 'Africa'. Virgin forests, majestic mountains surrounded by savannas, lush oases, vast empty plains marked by the rhythms of animal life, where lions, elephants, giraffes and rhinoceroses reign as lords of nature, far from civilization. All of us carry such images in our heads. Images suffused with a sense of eternity, a reassuring emotion in the face of the damage being inflicted everywhere else in the world by modernity – our modernity.

But this Africa does not exist. It has never existed and the problem is that we have convinced ourselves of the opposite. The more nature disappears in the West, the more we fantasize about it in Africa. The more we destroy nature *here*, the more energetically we try to save it *there*. With UNESCO, the WWF (formerly known as the World Wildlife Fund and then as the World Wide Fund for Nature) or the International Union for Conservation of Nature (IUCN), we manage to convince ourselves that, in the African national parks, we are protecting the last vestiges of a world once untouched and wild.

In reality, these institutions are responsible for the rapid naturalization of large areas of the continent. By naturalization,

I am referring to the dehumanization of Africa, a process which involves turning territories into national parks, banning agriculture in these areas, evicting people from their homes and getting rid of their fields and grazing land in order to create a supposedly natural world, in which people are absent. And this battle for a phantom Africa has no impact whatsoever on the destruction of biodiversity. On the contrary, this process is proving to have disastrous effects on all of those living in the natural world. The enforced eviction of local people, fines, prison sentences, social breakdown, beatings, sometimes rapes and even murders: these are the catastrophic consequences of this westernized vision of Africa.

This book investigates the mechanisms of this violence. It describes the history and the ongoing reality of the injustice which continues to permeate the lives of those living in or near the African national parks.

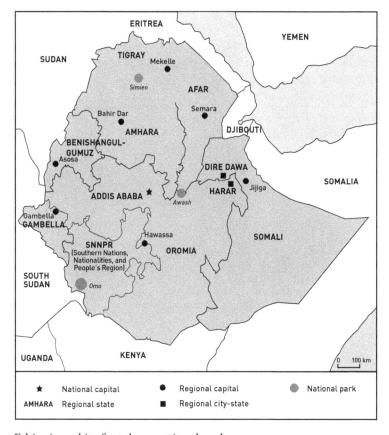

Ethiopia and its first three national parks

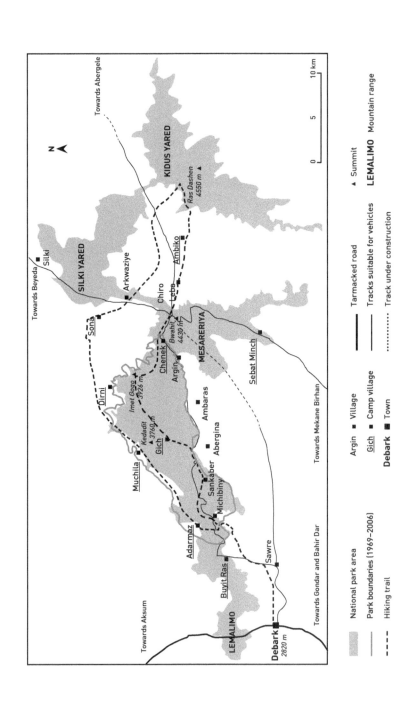

Towards Abergele

KIDUS YARED

Ras Dashen
4550 m ▲

SILKI YARED

Silki

Arkwaziye

Ambiko

Chiro

Leba

Towards Beyeda

Sona

Bwahit
4430 m ▲

Chenek

MESARERIYA

Argin

Sebat Minch

Dirni

Imet Gogo
3926 m ▲

Ambaras

Kedadit
3760 m ▲

Gich

Abergina

Muchila

Sankaber

Michibiny

Towards Mekane Birhan

Adarmaz

Towards Aksum

Buyit Ras

Sawre

LEMALIMO

Debark
2820 m

Towards Gondar and Bahir Dar

N

0   5   10 km

Argin ■ Village
Gich ■ Camp village
Debark ■ Town

Tarmacked road
Tracks suitable for vehicles
Track under construction

▲ Summit
LEMALIMO Mountain range

National park area
Park boundaries (1969–2006)
Hiking trail

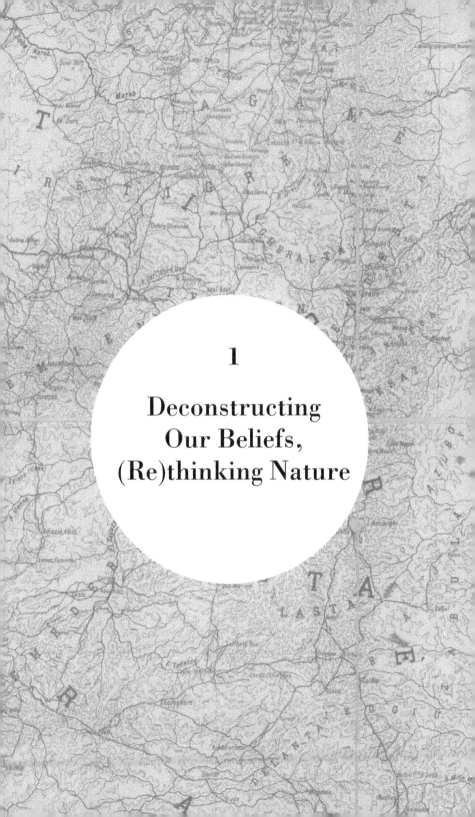

1

Deconstructing Our Beliefs, (Re)thinking Nature

4 January 2019, the suburbs of Debark, north of the Ethiopian highlands. Seated on a mattress on the bare ground, in a house constructed of wood and corrugated iron, Samson describes with bitterness the details of his everyday existence since his eviction: 'They drove us out with sticks. [. . .] They ordered us to leave in the name of UNESCO. [. . .] We just can't go on living like this. I feel as if I'm dying here.'[1]

The same feelings of despair have haunted Samson's neighbours since they were brought into the town on 16 June 2016. On that day, in the early hours of the morning, guards from the Simien National Park arrived in Gich, a village with a population of 2,508 inhabitants, perched at an altitude of 3,800 metres. The villagers were agro-pastoralists, which means they combined growing crops and raising livestock on pasture lands. As a result, they were accused of destroying nature. That is why the park guards ended up forcibly evicting them from their mountains. On the evening of 16 June, the entire population of Gich were resettled in Debark, a small town situated 35 kilometres further west, outside the boundaries of the Simien National Park.

The Ethiopian state had succeeded, at last. In 1978, UNESCO had placed the Simien National Park on its list of world heritage sites but, in 1996, the park was relegated to the List of World Heritage in Danger. According to international experts, the reason for this change was that by cultivating the land and raising livestock, the local people were damaging the natural environment.[2] Evicting them was seen as the solution to the problem, and, as a result, UNESCO offered its congratulations to Ethiopia, announcing on 12 July 2017 that the Simien National Park would be removed from the List of World Heritage in Danger.

The institution had yet another demand to make. Several thousand agro-pastoralists were still living in the park and UNESCO requested that they also be evicted. The Ethiopian leaders were ready to make this sacrifice because, as far as they were concerned, what mattered was to finally receive the reward for which they had waited twenty years: the reinstatement of the Simien Park on UNESCO's prestigious list of world heritage sites.[3]

This victory came at a single price: the village of Gich. On the day following the eviction, the other inhabitants of the park entered the village. They dismantled the houses abandoned by their former neighbours and took away with them the wood they needed for cooking and keeping warm. As for the former inhabitants of Gich, they would try to adjust to the urban lifestyle imposed upon them. With little success. 'I can't take any more,' Samson tells us, three years later. 'It's either death or a return to our land.'

Social injustice and ecological absurdity

It was thanks to Samson that I was able to find out more about this national park. That is not his real name, since for him, and for all the inhabitants cited in this book, caution requires that their anonymity be respected. In Paris, teachers at Inalco (Institut National des Langues et Civilisations Orientales) taught me the basics of Amharic, the Ethiopian *lingua franca*. In Addis Ababa and in Debark, officials from the EWCO (Ethiopian Wildlife Conservation Organization) granted me access to their entire archive – almost 20,000 pages of correspondence, minutes and progress reports. And, from 2007 onwards, the inhabitants of Simien have made me welcome in their mountains. On each of my visits there, they have helped me understand that living in the Simien Park means living illegally. Since cultivating the land and raising livestock are punishable by law, being born in a national park means being a squatter in your own home.

This story has revealed a world whose existence I did not even suspect. I thought that the African parks were harmonious natural spaces. Instead, I discovered whole areas undermined by violence.

I say 'the African parks' because the Simien is by no means an isolated case. There are around 350 national parks in Africa, and in most of them, local populations have been driven out in favour of either animals, forests or savannas. This is the case in 50% of parks in Benin, 40% of parks in Rwanda and 30% of parks in Tanzania and in the Democratic Republic of the Congo. Over the course of the twentieth century, at least a million people were driven out of protected zones in Africa.[4] And in those parks which are still inhabited, agriculture, pastoralism and hunting are largely forbidden and punishable by fines or prison sentences. It is not therefore Ethiopia's attitude to nature which constitutes an exception in the world, but rather the world's attitude to nature in Africa. For over a century, under the influence of experts from the North, this coercive naturalization of specific areas has affected every single country within the continent.

These environmental policies were devised by Europeans during the period of colonization. And, since independence, they have been implemented by individual African states. The leaders of these states have sovereignty yet they systematically bow to any orders imposed by the international conservation institutions.[5] Behind every incidence of social injustice imposed on those living in natural environments throughout Africa, the presence of UNESCO, the WWF, the IUCN or Flora & Fauna International (FFI) is never far away.

Such a claim is certainly surprising. Indeed, so powerfully does it go against what we have been led to believe that some people refuse even to contemplate it. It should therefore be made clear at once that this book does not set out to denigrate the environmental cause or to criticize the ecological battle. On the contrary, this work hopes to participate actively in these processes. If the worldwide destruction of biodiversity is to be avoided, it is imperative that we understand our mistakes.

As political scientist Luc Semal explains, African societies will be forced to face the collapse of their ecosystems just as is already the case in Europe, America and Asia. Specializing in environmental movements and a leading expert in animal extinctions,[6] Semal highlights the weight of anxiety provoked by the now very real prospect of the ecological and human disasters which are threatening to erupt on a worldwide scale under the cumulative effects of global warming, dwindling resources and the disappearance of certain species of fauna and flora.[7] Yet the expulsion of inhabitants from African national parks will in no circumstances provide a solution to any of these problems. Quite the contrary, any notion that confining nature within parks is a better way of protecting the planet is a delusion. And, by nourishing that delusion, international conservation policies constitute a kind of optical illusion which effectively hides the real problem: the massive and worldwide deterioration of 'our' everyday environment.

In order to save nature, international experts insist that African states must evict those living within the national parks. In concrete terms, they want them to prevent agro-pastoralists from eroding the strips of land they cultivate and from stripping bare the plateaux where they allow their cattle to graze. But the argument is a nonsense in the true sense of the word – it goes against reason. Accusing peasants, like those from Gich, of destroying nature fails to acknowledge that these people are in fact producing their own food. Like all those evicted from the African national parks, they move around essentially on foot. They eat very little meat and fish. They rarely buy new clothes. And, unlike two billion individuals, they own neither computers nor smartphones. In short, if we want to save the planet, we should live as they do. Yet UNESCO, the WWF and the IUCN nevertheless view their eviction as ethical and necessary, in other words just and justified. Why?

Green colonialism

As current events are beginning to demonstrate, the whole issue of worldwide ecology is influenced by the colonial past. In August 2019, for example, when French president Emmanuel Macron suggested that the fires burning in Amazonia should be placed under international control, Jair Bolsonaro was quick to condemn 'a colonialist mentality'. 'Macron [. . .] wants to "save" Amazonia as though it were [still] a colony,' wrote the Brazilian president on his Twitter account.[8]

At the same time, in the context of Africa, a controversy erupted in the United States after the release of the new film version of *The Lion King*. Millions of spectators flocked to rediscover the Disney characters, with voiceovers recorded by Afro-American artists – including the singer Beyoncé and the actor Donald Glover. The remake met with worldwide success but a number of intellectuals condemned what they saw as a 'perfectly colonial' film. According to them, *The Lion King* perpetuates the notion of an Africa which is more about nature than it is about human beings. In such a context, Africans would have no place in their own continent but would instead be intruders whose presence disturbed the equilibrium of a green planet.[9]

Nor did Asia escape such clichés. In October 2019, *Le Monde* devoted a special report to the rise of eco-fascism. The French daily turned its attention in particular to the massacre in Christchurch, New Zealand, carried out by an Australian extreme-right activist. A few minutes before killing fifty-one Muslims in two different mosques, Brenton Tarrant published a manifesto on social media networks: '[T]he environment is being destroyed by overpopulation, we Europeans are one of the groups that are not overpopulating the world.' For all those who, like him, consider themselves eco-fascists, the message is clear: 'Kill the invaders, kill the overpopulation and by doing so save the environment.'[10]

Such extremists are not alone in believing they have been charged with a mission. According to other media sources, many international experts also suffer from a neo-Malthusian anxiety. They set themselves the task of saving nature in all the countries in the southern hemisphere before ecologically irresponsible local inhabitants end up destroying it.

In this respect, the written press in particular targets the WWF. In 2012, in *PandaLeaks*, the journalist Wilfried Huismann exposed the role played by the WWF in the forced expulsions of indigenous populations from national parks in Africa and Asia.[11] In 2016, the association Survival International in turn launched an attack on the WWF, accusing it of financing the military campaigns of the Cameroon government against tribes living in the protected forests in the south of the country.[12] Finally, both *BuzzFeed News* and *Mediapart* condemned what they refer to as 'green colonialism'. In 2019, they claimed that the WWF was training and arming guards who then beat, raped and sometimes killed women and men accused of poaching. According to both these websites, such atrocities are the common lot of several national parks in India, Nepal, Gabon and the Congo – in short, in the former European colonies.[13]

The link between colonial geography and the current policies of an international institution like the WWF is glaringly obvious, even flagrant. But the situation is also more complex than it appears and the media struggle to furnish a clear explanation of what green colonialism really is. For that, we need to turn back to history.

The story began in North America, at the end of the nineteenth century. The United States and Canada created the first national parks in the world and, in each case, local people were evicted. The two countries (re)introduced supposedly authentic animal species, (re)planted supposedly original forests and (re)seeded supposedly natural plains. Then, once these tasks had been successfully accomplished, they turned their attention to making nature in its wild state – the wilderness – into a national symbol. In each national park, nature became the nation's soul. It was described to the public as the authentic essence of the two societies, the original face of two countries which were shaped from the collective experience of a wild and uninhabited landscape, and not out of the violence of a colonial conquest.

At the beginning of the 1930s, this enthusiasm for national parks spread to Europe. European governments rarely expelled the inhabitants of their parks. Although they, too, were exploiting the concept of nature, their approach was different. Rather than creating a virgin and timeless wilderness, they chose to highlight the link between their nations and a nature which has been humanized since time immemorial. For example, in Switzerland, the mountain pastures were transformed into sacred ground, the symbol of land which had been farmed in the same way over the course of many centuries by the people of one and the same nation, irrespective of any differences between them. In a similar vein, Germany set about making its forests and their folklore into the symbol of the smaller homelands (*Heimat*) where the local people could learn to love the greater fatherland (*Vaterland*).

The process is therefore the same as in North America. Everywhere they appeared, national parks encouraged an extension from the local to the national, from local park to the nation which protects it, from the love of a small area to the love of a much more extensive one, as so eloquently described by the historian François Walter.[14]

During the mid-1960s, it was the turn of France to adopt the model. The France of small farmers and peasants was in the process of vanishing and the state was in quest of some form of substitute for the rural identity of the nation.[15] As a result, in the national parks of the Vanoise, the Pyrenees or the Mercantour, park authorities saw their mission as that of 'restoring the ecological balance of such places'. They banned the industrialization of agriculture, (re)naturalized ecosystems with high-altitude grassland in some cases, or peat bogs in others, and (re)introduced animal species, including wild vultures, black grouse and ibex. According to the French government, such an approach would guarantee the 'natural return of species of particular interest in terms of national heritage'.[16]

This return to the past was, however, by no means natural. Nor was it particularly objective. In the rivers of the Cévennes National Park, for example, the park administration reintroduced beavers on the basis of their 'authenticity', even though they had disappeared from the region in the fourteenth century. By contrast, no operation on a similar scale was envisaged to combat the disappearance of grey partridges or wolves. Less emblematic or more dangerous, these species nevertheless disappeared barely a century ago.

Such subjectivity regarding authenticity is all the more flagrant when we see how, in France, park authorities protect what they describe as 'the character of the site'. They renovate traditional sheep pens. They rent out land to agro-pastoralists who, thanks to reduced rents, can continue to live there. They maintain transhumance routes and, at the beginning of the summer, pay out subsidies to those shepherds who agree to undertake their transhumance on foot, and not in a truck, as is the case elsewhere in France. They subsidize local crafts and also train young adults in skills relating to what are considered to be ancestral architectural techniques. In short, in France, as elsewhere, the park authorities transform nature into what they believe it once was.[17]

The situation is much the same on the other side of the Mediterranean. But the perception of how the natural environment used to be is very different indeed. Africa was virgin territory and must remain so. Rather than shaping the environment as Europeans have done, Africans destroy it. In order to gain a clearer picture of the situation, let us continue to focus our attention on France. Since 2011, the Cévennes National Park has been classified as a UNESCO World Heritage Site. According to the UNESCO website, the Cévennes is an area of 'outstanding universal value'. A value which comes from 'landscapes [. . .] shaped by agro-pastoralism over three millennia'. The aim, UNESCO explains, is to save 'the agro-pastoral systems' of the Cévennes, and 'to maintain these through the perpetuation of traditional activities'.[18]

This description may seem unremarkable. Yet in comparison with the UNESCO description of the Simien National Park in Ethiopia it is nevertheless striking. Situated at altitudes of between 2,800 and 4,600 metres, with a surface area of 410 square kilometres (four times the size of Paris), the park is a mountainous landscape which closely resembles that of the Cévennes. The area has a moderately dense population living in scattered hamlets, valleys dotted with terraces dedicated to food production, and pasture lands used for subsistence farming. Yet the 'universal value' of the Simien has nothing to do with any of this. Instead, according to UNESCO, it comes in the form of the area's 'spectacular landscape' and in the presence of 'globally threatened species, including the iconic Walia ibex, a wild mountain goat found nowhere else in the world'.

As for the inhabitants of the Simien National Park, agro-pastoralists like those in the Cévennes, their presence seems to be far from appreciated. On the contrary, writes UNESCO, 'Agricultural and pastoral activities [. . .] have severely affected the natural values of the property.' Even today, the institution informs us, again on its website, 'Threats to the integrity of the park include human settlement, cultivation and soil erosion.'[19]

In response to the same type of agro-pastoral space, one in France and the other in Ethiopia, UNESCO nevertheless comes up with two radically different stories. The first one is European and depicts humankind's adaptation to nature. The second is African and recounts the damage inflicted on nature by humankind. This version of events brings with it serious consequences. As early as 1963, experts from UNESCO, the IUCN and the WWF were recommending that Ethiopia should transform the Simien area into a national park. And, in order for that to happen, they asked Ethiopia to 'extinguish all individual or other human rights'.[20] The same request led to Ethiopia evicting the inhabitants of Gich in 2016. In Africa, a national park must be empty.

This ideal of nature stripped of its inhabitants is the guiding force behind the majority of protected zones within the continent. This is the essence of green colonialism. During the colonial era, there was the 'white man's burden', the supposed civilizational duty of the white man, with its racist theories justifying the domination of Africans. Then came the ecological burden of the western expert with declinist environmental theories legitimizing control of Africa. The intention may no longer be the same, but the spirit remains identical: the modern and civilized world must continue to save Africa from the Africans.

Understanding Africa through Ethiopian history

Faced with this situation, two challenges present themselves. First, we need to understand why the colonial past weighs so heavily on the present. Why, at the end of the nineteenth century, did European 'scientists' convince themselves that Africa was an Eden in the throes of being destroyed? How was is that, at the beginning of the 1960s, this myth still persisted under the influence of colonial administrators, now transformed into international experts? Finally, what kind of logic has, over a period of thirty years, driven major international institutions to prioritize local and participative management of nature, while at the same time clamouring, time and time again, for the eviction of local populations?

We need to turn to history, therefore, but also to geography. Western literature generally portrays Africa as one big homogeneous whole. With the Hutu and Tutsi people, Rwanda and Burundi share the same history. Formerly Northern and Southern Rhodesia, Zambia and Zimbabwe are more or less identical. Congo-Kinshasa and Congo-Brazzaville are, of course, much alike. This denial of individual identity has led me to construct this book around one area in particular: Ethiopia. I have chosen this country because it is marked just as much by western interference as by endogenous nationalism, two contradictory forces which are present in all the states in the continent, though to different degrees. The book features only those Ethiopian events which might be applicable to other African countries. Each chapter establishes a link between Ethiopian history and African history. But rather than taking a superficial overview of the continent, our starting point will be the Ethiopian archives and a view from ground level, from where it is genuinely possible to understand social life, in Africa, and all over the world.

Ethiopia offers a perspective which is all the more interesting in that the country has never been colonized. It is the only state in the continent to have escaped European domination, and yet, in spite of this, it is as much affected by green colonialism as its neighbours.

The history of modern-day Ethiopia is marked by four separate phases. First of all came the conquests of Menelik II, king of kings of Ethiopia from 1889 to 1913. When the colonization of Africa began, Menelik's Christian kingdom was confined to the high central plateaux of present-day Ethiopia, the equivalent of just half of the country. Then, gradually, his kingdom became surrounded by Europeans, with British Kenya to the south, Italian Somalia and French Somaliland (Djibouti) further to the east, Italian Eritrea to the north and British Sudan to the west. Only a handful of sultanates and some minor African monarchies separated Ethiopia from these colonies, and if the Europeans succeeded in subjugating them, they would find themselves on the threshold of Menelik's kingdom. But, against all the odds, the king of kings ended up victorious. Taking advantage of the rivalries between the various European factions, his army successfully invaded all the regions adjoining his kingdom, one after the other. As a result, Ethiopia became a colonial power – but an African one.

Haile Selassie succeeded Menelik II as the leader of this Greater Ethiopia. With the exception of the period of Italian occupation (1936–41), he led the country from 1930 to 1974. As emperor, he imposed a Christian Orthodox culture and a single language, Amharic. Haile Selassie also deployed the classic tools of the nation-state. He established a central administration, a flag and a national anthem and then organized the construction of national museums and the classification of historical monuments. His goal was to unite all the peoples conquered by Menelik under a *national* identity, and a single *Ethiopian* state.

As a consequence of his overly zealous drive to Ethiopianize his subjects, in 1974, Haile Selassie was overthrown by the soldiers of the Derg (committee). His remains would be discovered some years later under the office of Mengistu Haile Mariam, the strongman behind the Derg. Thanks to the support of the USSR, Mengistu succeeded in imposing a Marxist-Leninist regime. He nationalized land, collectivized agriculture and successfully suppressed any opposition. Then, as in the days of the empire, the Derg also initiated a programme of Ethiopianization. By introducing free education, protecting a shared historical heritage and increasingly resorting to force, it set about nationalizing those populations which had been part of Greater Ethiopia at the beginning of the twentieth century.

It was the same policy as that pursued under the empire and, inevitably, it met with the same failure. In 1991, the Ethiopian People's Revolutionary Democratic Front overthrew the Derg. Under Meles Zenawi, prime minister until 2012, the new Federal Democratic Republic of Ethiopia introduced a market economy. This proved so successful that the country became one of the major powers of the continent. Yet national cohesion remained out of reach. The people of the Oromo, Afar or Somalia had been conquered by Menelik a century earlier and, very often, they still refused to accept the Ethiopian identity which the country's leaders sought to impose on them.

A similar phenomenon can be observed in many African countries. The western press and observers attribute this lack of unity to ethnic divisions. But 'ethnicity' is a category invented by Europeans during colonization to impose submission on the kingdoms they were invading. And since then, ethnicism has continued to cast an air of otherness over the whole of Africa: where France had its *peoples* (3 million Bretons), Ethiopia had its ethnic groups (40 million Oromo). In reality, the word conceals a far simpler story. The colonial frontiers ended up bringing about a superficial regrouping of peoples who are very different from each other – it is as straightforward as that.

From the start of independence to the beginning of the 1960s, African states therefore found themselves doing what western governments had done at the end of the nineteenth century. In order to give substance to the idea of the nation, they created a national story, identified national heroes, built national monuments or rallied around national football teams. And they created national parks. As in the United States, Germany or Switzerland, each African state elevated its parks to the status of national shrines. These natural spaces were intended to allow people to fully experience their country, to admire it and to love it.

Nevertheless, two radically different approaches separate Africa from Europe and North America. Today, in almost every African national park, people are still being evicted and criminalized. And in all these places, this oppression of local people is led by those employed by the international conservation institutions with, at the top of the list, UNESCO, the IUCN and the WWF. It is these two faces of African nature – the international experts, on the one hand, and, on the other, the local inhabitants who are the target of their prejudices – that lie at the heart of this book

Our story therefore draws on history more by necessity than by choice. From the colonial invention of the African Eden to the postcolonial construct imposed by the experts, from the African use of international norms to the myth of sustainable development, only the past can enable us to understand why, even today, western conservationists are intent on making Africa wild, no matter what the cost.

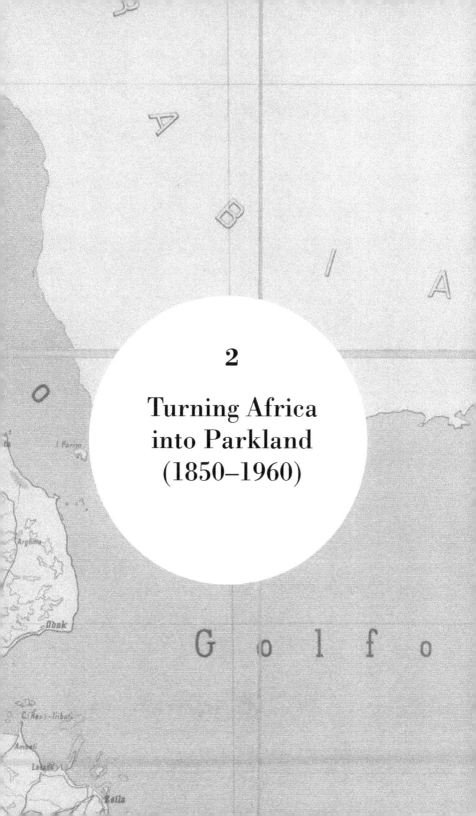

2

Turning Africa
into Parkland
(1850–1960)

Paris, March 2017. The French edition of *National Geographic* magazine publishes a guide to the most beautiful national parks in the world. Continent by continent, the famous monthly invites us to embark on a veritable world tour.

First of all, North America. In the land of canyons and great lakes, the magazine tells us, quoting President Franklin Roosevelt: 'The fundamental idea behind the parks . . . is that the country belongs to the people.' In Asia, too, a special bond exists between the people and their parks. In this continent with a thousand mountains, each summit has its Nepalese flags, its Hindu temple or its monastery. Humans are everywhere; discreet but omnipresent. This interaction between humankind and the environment pales into insignificance, however, in comparison with Europe. Here, according to the magazine, the most modest landscape spells out the harmony between nature and farming: 'charming villages, rugged moorlands and ancient castles perched on cliffs'.

And then there is Africa. There, the *National Geographic* explains, it is the natural world that reigns supreme: 'The African parks pulse with an energy generated by rolling savannas, lush jungles, spectacular waterfalls and, of course, the extraordinary fauna. [. . .] This ancient continent takes us back in time to the very source of the history of the earth as we discover rivers and grasslands from which, long ago, sprang much of the life of our planet.'[1]

An Eden of fauna, flora and panoramas, but never of people. This is Africa as described to more than 40 million readers throughout the world. But why this image? Can the African parks never be an object of national pride as they are in the United States, or even the focus of particular religious practice as in Asia? Is nature in Africa somehow so different to nature as found in Europe? In order to understand this fantastical vision of Africa, we need to travel back through time, from the age of great discoveries to the end of the colonial era.

Eden and its fall

In the sixteenth century, navigators, geographers and scholars from all over Europe were in quest of Eden. They were convinced that by sailing the oceans they would end up finding it, somewhere on this earth. Not surprisingly, their quest met with failure. It did, however, enable them to discover islands with luxuriant vegetation, to experience nature as never seen before, in the Canaries, the Mascarene Islands, St Helena, Mauritius. These paradise islands would be their Eden and they set about colonizing them over the course of the seventeenth century.

The problem was that colonization and the natural environment are incompatible. One after the other, from the Atlantic to the Indian Ocean, these natural oases were subjected to repeated assaults by the European plantation economy. They also served as supply stations for the ships of the British, Dutch, French and Portuguese East India companies. The growing need for wood, water and food required more and more land to be exploited. No sooner was it discovered, therefore, than the longed-for Eden was lost. The more the colonization pro-gramme advanced, the more the paradise islands inevitably deteriorated.

During the course of the eighteenth century, naturalists, botanists and agronomists began to be aware of the scale of the catastrophe. They alerted colonial governors and, at the begin-ning of the nineteenth century, these administrators set in place the first conservation measures of our era. They initiated programmes of reforestation, created forestry reserves and oversaw the construction of large-scale irrigation infrastruc-tures. As far as the authorities were concerned, these policies did indeed have an ecological interest, but there was more to it than that. For, rather than pointing the finger at their own forms of exploitation, the colonists accused the 'natives' of destroying nature. And, as a consequence, they deprived them of the right to cultivate the land.[2]

The same process was repeated after 1850, when coloniza-tion extended all the way from the tropics to Africa. Initially, this brought with it romanticism and adventure.

Europe was in the throes of the industrial revolution. Cities and factories were gradually eating away at the countryside, rural landscapes were being eroded at an alarming rate and anxiety levels were rising amongst the elite. Mountaineers, painters, writers and intellectuals were the direct descendants of romanticism. Their mission was to save the authentic char-acter of the world before it was too late. In every corner of the ancient continent, they campaigned therefore for the protec-tion of any native species still spared by technological progress.

Their passion for a non-urban and non-industrialized world meant that they, too, turned their attention to Africa. European romantics saw it as a sanctuary for the wildlife that was being eradicated at home, and which was threatened with the same fate in Africa, too, as a consequence of the damage inflicted by that continent's primitive inhabitants.[3]

The popular press fuelled this vision by publishing countless travel journals and accounts. Explorers, scientists or traders, both Europeans and Americans, were fascinated by Africa. They explored it and, once home, wrote about their experience. Stanley's encounter with Dr Livingstone took place in Tanganyika in 1871 and by 1872 he was describing 'enchanting scenery', 'spontaneous growth' and how 'the foulness [of malaria] might be removed by civilized people, and the whole region made as healthy as it is productive'.[4] Thirty years later, Winston Churchill and Theodore Roosevelt were depicting the same Africa. Taking Uganda as their starting point, they combined the pleasures of hunting with those of safari. In 1907, Churchill described the landscape as 'zoological gardens', and Roosevelt, in 1909, called it a 'vast zoological garden [. . .] where these savages are . . . wastefully destructive of the forests'.[5]

The success of these accounts was all the more resounding in that they echoed those emanating from scholars specializing in the Orient. The ultimate in erudite science, orientalism was, to paraphrase Edward Said, establishing itself as a western form of domination. Americans and Europeans were describing Africa and Asia in terms of childlike and unformed versions of western civilization, which was seen to be mature, modern and developed. The human sciences and travel literature then inspired a genuine outpouring of imagery focusing on the Other and the Elsewhere. The West defined its identity by setting itself apart from an Africa which had conserved its natural state, and from Africans who continued to live in a primitive manner.[6]

The ecological impact of colonization

It should be pointed out that a number of bio-political catastrophes helped to reinforce this vision. Between 1888 and 1892, from East Africa to South Africa, Europeans imported bullocks, probably from India. But the bullocks were infected with cattle plague. The infection spread rapidly and entire breeding herds were wiped out. Local populations lost their draught animals and crops failed. A period of drought aggravated the situation still further and an ensuing plague of locusts destroyed any reserves. The price of cereals rocketed and famines were wide-spread. People fled the affected areas and the savannas became more extensive. As a result, when Europeans who had set out to try their luck in the colonies came upon these deserted landscapes, their notion of Africa was confirmed: clearly, the continent was still in a completely natural state.[7]

The colonists were also convinced that the Africans were responsible for the disappearance of wildlife. Faced with the various catastrophes which were destroying their crops, African farmers were left with little choice. In order to survive, they were forced to resort to hunting big game such as buffalo, zebras and lions. From a European perspective, this kind of hunting was further evidence of the savagery of the colonized populations. Yet, by linking Africa to new worldwide trade routes, it was in fact colonization itself which was responsible for the intensification of hunting. At the end of the nineteenth century, for example, European and African hunters were kill-ing 65,000 elephants per year for the ivory trade. They sold the ivory to Europeans and Americans, who in turn supplied them with textiles and arms, with the help of Arabic and Swahili middlemen.

The railway proved to be another source of predation. European workers laid the tracks and, all along the route, their employers fed them on locally hunted meat. Moreover, they were often joined by European naturalists. These were unrestrained collectors of wildlife specimens: in 1895, in May alone, one ornithologist killed sixty zebras, which he sent to the Museum of Natural History in Berlin. Finally, the colonial armies and administrators relished opportunities to hunt for sport. It gave them an opportunity to demonstrate their masculinity and their ability to dominate nature.[8]

This unbridled exploitation of the environment was equally detrimental to both wildlife and soil within the continent. The Africans had exploited the forests long before the arrival of the Europeans. But with the expansion of trade, transport systems and agriculture, colonization triggered an unprecedented deforestation. Between 1850 and 1920, in sub-Saharan Africa and in South-East Asia, 94 million hectares of forests were destroyed and the land turned over to farmland. This figure was between four and five times greater than in the whole of the previous century.[9] As had been the case in the tropical islands during the eighteenth century, Europeans failed to recognize the fact that it was their presence which was causing the ecological devastation they were witnessing. On the contrary, as far as they were concerned, the blame lay with the Africans.

The myths underpinning colonialism

Here, too, scientists played a crucial role. At the beginning of the twentieth century, taxonomists, zoologists and foresters became the advance guard of the colonial effort. Thanks to their findings, European powers were able to classify African ecosystems, demarcate natural regions and maximize the exploitation of these areas.

Some of these scientists based their information on knowledge obtained from local people, without necessarily treating these with contempt. They proved, however, to be incapable of overcoming their prejudices. They lacked data from which to study a continent which was still only partially explored, but they were nevertheless convinced that the 'natives' did not have the technical skills needed to use their resources correctly. Their knowledge was as incomplete as it was biased and yet the colonial governors continued to rely on the information they provided. With good reason, for science provided Europe with the necessary legitimacy to exploit Africa, and to expropriate the African people.[10]

It was in this context that the myth of 'primary' forests first emerged. At the beginning of the twentieth century, French botanists studying the rural environment of West Africa came upon villages surrounded by a narrow belt of forestry with savanna extending between them on all sides. Under the influence of the climax theory, they were convinced that a dense and extensive forest had once existed where there was now only savanna. These narrow forest belts were therefore taken as evidence of the damage caused by the Africans. First there was the virgin forest; then humans came along and set about clearing the forests; finally came the villages surrounded by the few surviving trees.

This myth became ubiquitous. Yet the botanists had read history backwards. In semi-arid environments, tree belts are not the vestiges of a primary forest which humans have hacked back and parcelled out. On the contrary, in the majority of cases, these are the result of human activity: first there is the soil stripped almost bare, then farming is introduced to fertilize the soil and create low-lying shrubs and, finally, the savanna fires result in a forest cover which, though never abundant, is rarely exhausted.

The more people there are, the more forests there will be. This is what generally happens. Contrary to the claims made by European scientists, in the majority of African ecologies, rural people have not destroyed their environment. Instead, they have adapted to it by creating forests which then provided them with firewood and timber for building.

A somewhat similar error fuelled the desertification narrative. In the Maghreb, during the 1920s, botanists and foresters concluded that slash-and-burn farming and pastoralism had completely dried out the soil. The colonial government acted on their analyses and their advice. It converted forestry land into public property, forced nomadic people to settle and expropriated farmers. But, in reality, the majority of plants in the desert are adapted to both fire and grazing. Moreover, some of them are even dependent on them and will die if they are not regularly burned or grazed. And, even in cases of extreme drought, this unique vegetation will grow back again, thanks to the seed stocks buried in arid soils.

Nor do deserts spread as rapidly as is often believed. They expand and shrink depending on rainfall, and this happens over a long period – as the Sahara has demonstrated over 65 million years. It should also be pointed out that the (re)forestation of desert areas always ends in failure. In the rare cases where the trees planted manage to survive, they fail to attract the desired rainfall amounts – only topography and climate are capable of increasing rainfall. Instead, these trees drain moisture from the water table, the wells and the soil. In reality, reforestation causes the quality of arable lands to deteriorate.[11]

By the end of the 1920s, the environment in the Maghreb was in urgent need of protection. Intensive agriculture had restricted soil recovery by shortening the fallow period. Converted into agricultural land, seasonal grazing areas had become dried out. And the army's demand for wood had left the forests decimated.

But in the Maghreb, as in Africa, colonial scientists and administrators remained convinced that it was the 'natives' who were responsible for destroying nature. They had no figures from the period prior to colonization, nor any overall statistics for the colonial period. So why did they still believe in this declinist narrative? The answer lies in the fact that colonization is based on the civilizing mission of Europeans, on the pressing need to export their ways of doing things into Africa. Putting the blame on the colonized peoples was therefore a way of reassuring the authorities about the validity of the colonial system.[12] By shifting the responsibility for the damage caused by the Europeans onto the Africans, the government and the colonists could continue to deny the evidence: in order to save nature, they needed to protect it from capitalism, their capitalism.[13]

From game reserves to national parks

Within the game reserves, the contradiction is glaring. With the inclusion of Africa in a worldwide illegal wildlife trade, animal numbers declined dramatically. And, in response, from 1892 onwards, the British and the Germans began to create reserves in their East African colonies. They established hunting seasons, imposed the compulsory purchase of hunting permits and forbade many hunting practices.

In doing so, they were reproducing the aristocratic model of modern Europe in Africa. From that point on, an entire arsenal of legislative measures distinguished the good 'hunter' from the bad 'poacher': the white elite who valiantly hunted for trophies with guns from the Africans who killed animals cruelly with the aid of nets, bows and spears. These game reserves therefore represented a triple advantage for the colonial authorities. They allowed them to accumulate revenue, to tighten their control over the illegal wildlife trade amongst European hunters and to restrict the access of Africans to their own resources.[14]

As for the animals, as the historian Violette Pouillard so elegantly puts it, these nature reserves meant that their protectors were now also the people who were killing them. The Europeans created reserves in all their colonies and, in the spring of 1900, Great Britain, Germany, Spain, Belgium, France, Italy and Portugal organized a conference on the preservation of African species which was scheduled to take place in London. The British were careful to wait until the end of April before convening the delegates of the imperial powers. The hunting season was coming to an end in East Africa, and all the 'experts' would therefore be back in time to draw up the Convention for the Preservation of Wild Animals, Birds and Fish in Africa. This convention would never be officially ratified but, until the end of the 1920s, it allowed the colonial powers to define a common policy within their reserves. The Whites could continue to hunt, and the Africans would be evicted, or at least deprived of a good many of their existing rights.[15]

The conference also enabled an international network of conservationists to be set up. This included trophy hunters, colonial administrators and specimen collectors from Britain, Germany, Belgium, Italy and France. They were centred on the British Society for the Preservation of the Wild Fauna of the Empire (SPWFE), and later on the highly elitist Shikar Club, reserved only for those hunters who had distinguished themselves across all three continents of Africa, Asia and Europe.

This passion for hunting would earn these conservation-ists the nickname of 'penitent butchers'. They had spent their youth killing the greatest wildlife species in existence, and in their view, the reserves should from then on become places of ethical equilibrium: a regulated European hunting ground in which the game would not be threatened with extinction; and a restrictive conservation which would protect wildlife from the cruelty of the Africans.[16]

These penitent butchers next set about campaigning in sup-port of sanctuaries entirely dedicated to animal life. Thanks to their influence within the colonies, the hunting reserves were then converted into national parks. The first of these, Albert Park (now Virunga Park), was created in the Belgian Congo in 1925. The following year, the South African reserve in the Transvaal province became the Kruger Park. And, in 1928, the empires established this paradigm across the whole of Africa by creating the International Office of Documentation and Correlation for the Protection of Nature (l'Office international de documentation et de correlation pour la protection de la nature). This provided a network of communication between the major cities of Europe and their colonies.

Finally, in 1933, Great Britain organized a second international conference. Once again, colonial governors, naturalists and former hunters-turned-field scientists gathered together in London. The result was the Convention Relative to the Preservation of Flora and Fauna in Their Natural State, and this time the European governments officially adopted a 'special regime for the preservation of fauna and flora'. This regime, the Convention states, would be implemented in the national parks, in which 'the hunting, killing or capturing of fauna, and the collection or destruction of flora shall be limited or prohibited'.[17]

Nature idealized and exploited

The era of the national parks had begun, underpinned by the image of an African nature in its virgin and wild state. In 1936, with *The Snows of Kilimanjaro*, Hemingway transported western readers to a fairy-tale Africa. There, they discovered a landscape 'as wide as all the world', where the 'big five' reigned supreme: the lion, the leopard, the elephant, the buffalo and the black rhinoceros.[18] From 1937 onwards, western readers could also immerse themselves in the universe of an African farm and its owner, Karen Blixen. In *Out of Africa*, the Danish author depicted the life, in Kenya, of 'a person who had come from a rushed and noisy world into a still country'. This distant land was also evoked by many artists and in various different media. And all of these described a continent where humankind and nature had become one, an Eden where, as Blixen writes, 'The old dark clear-eyed Native of Africa, and the old dark clear-eyed elephant – they are alike; [. . .] they are themselves features of the land.'[19]

The more Europeans continued to deplete nature in Africa, the more they fantasized about it. Since the Great Depression of 1929, the colonists had extended their farmlands in order to compensate for the collapse in agricultural prices. And, in order to supply Europe, the colonial governments turned to Africa to source the raw materials which were lacking at home. The soil declined in quality and European administrators once again turned to science. Led by the British, they instigated major ecological studies with a view to modernizing their agricultural techniques across the entire continent. Foresters perfected their silvicultural methods, agronomists rationalized the use of agro-pastoral lands and all these colonial scientists continued to accuse the Africans of destroying the environment.

Poised between ecology and capitalism, this argument fuelled a desperate fear of erosion. In the United States, throughout the 1930s, dust storms had repeatedly hit the Great Plains, which were already over-farmed and eroded in the south of the country. The resulting Dust Bowl forced thousands of farmers off their land and many found themselves crowded into makeshift shanty towns. Consequently, when Sahelian Africa was struck by drought during the same period, Europeans took fright. If something similar to the American episode were to happen in their colonies, the peoples they had colonized might well rebel. Anticipatory measures were called for, and all over Africa, authorities set up commissions to study the phenomenon.[20]

The resulting surveys were, of course, localized. Yet it was very much an 'African' theory which began to emerge. For example, in 1939, British scientists Graham Jacks and Robert Whyte published a survey with the shocking title *The Rape of the Earth*. These specialists in soil science based their study on research carried out in 1919 in an area of British South Africa. In spite of the limited scope of their inquiry, they drew on the figures from South Africa to claim that the agro-pastoral techniques used by 'native' farmers were responsible for the 'Great

African Desert' which was forming across the whole continent. Each colonial state relied on reports of this kind. And, all over Africa, instead of reducing the impact of the colonial economy, the Europeans limited the individual and collective property rights of local people even more severely.[21]

Accepting that erosion exists is one thing; stating that it is a widespread threat is simply untrue. As is the declinist narrative which accompanies the increase in numbers of national parks across the continent, and according to which nature must be protected from destructive local populations. Every year, until the end of the 1940s, the colonial authorities were still handing out hundreds of hunting dispensations to colonists and to European scientists. For the Africans, however, the national parks had become veritable strongholds of conservation. Agriculture, pastoralism and occupation of the areas were punished ever more severely by the law, and the animal kingdom was from then on reserved for the exclusive delectation of the colonial elites.[22]

This penalization of colonized populations went hand in hand with another phenomenon, namely the anthropomorphizing of big game animals. European writers were the first to give African animals a more human face than they gave its inhabitants. In *The Roots of Heaven*, for example, Romain Gary describes the crusade of Morel, a young Frenchman, determined to save African elephants from extinction. 'A man can't spend his life in Africa', he says, 'without acquiring something pretty close to a great affection for the elephants.' But his attachment to animals does not extend to the inhabitants. For Morel, '[T]he one thing the natives see in an elephant is meat.'[23]

Four years later, in 1960, Joy Adamson published her autobiographical novel *Born Free*. From her home in British Kenya, the naturalist also tells two very different stories. First there are the Africans, always anonymous, unknown, and then there is Elsa, the young lioness Adamson adopted. Unlike the

Africans, Elsa has a name. The lioness also has feelings. She is playful, sometimes sad, in need of affection. And always freedom-loving. Rapidly adapted for the cinema, *Born Free* was a phenomenal success – a success enhanced by the fact that documentary films were at the same time enabling people in the West to discover animal society in Africa. Audiences learned, for example, that for elephants, life is governed by codified romantic relationships, funeral rituals and power struggles.[24]

Television then reinforced this naturalized vision of African social life with, in particular, the series *Jungle Emperor Leo*, adapted from Japanese mangas written by Osamu Tezuka between 1950 and 1954. Broadcast at the beginning of the 1960s, the series portrays the death of a lion and the combat waged by his young heir, king Leo, against the hyenas who are devastating the African savanna. The struggles of this lion king would provide inspiration for Disney – Africa is a green planet threatened by destructive beings.[25]

The image of a natural Africa gained strength, as did that of an overpopulated Africa. The colonized populations demanded the right to exploit their resources, and the new international institutions focused their anxieties on the Population Bomb. With the help of experts from the European empires, they formulated the concept of 'environmental security'. The principle is a simple one. If the third world had indeed just been set free, what Malthus had predicted two centuries earlier would now become reality: poor and overcrowded, people would consume resources until a worldwide conflict was triggered. And this time the danger would come from the demographic growth within Africa (thanks to the improvement in their living standards), and not from the European industries which were exporting wood, rubber and minerals back to their home countries.[26]

On the contrary, the modernization of these industries was seen as the solution to all evils. The imperial powers were convinced that with a colonial government backed by technology, they would be able to meet the needs both of the home countries in the process of reconstruction, and of those living under colonial rule. 'Development' therefore became the rationale behind a second colonial occupation: for the good of everyone, the Europeans needed to stay in Africa.[27]

The conservationists were directly involved in this undertaking. In each colony, European scientists and engineers were drawing up plans for the resettlement of local people. Their objective was to rationalize land use. The means chosen to achieve this involved attributing a productive function to each territory and then defining an appropriate population density. It was in this context that the eviction of inhabitants and the enforced reduction of livestock became standard practice within the national parks.

At a conference in Nairobi in 1947, the game wardens of the national parks in British Africa claimed that local people had killed 75% of the wildlife within the continent's parks. This allegation was not supported by any data. No specific parks were identified, nor were any specific species named. There was just this percentage, which was then sent to all the governors of British eastern and central Africa. The imperial authorities urged them to increase the number of parks and reinforce legislation in them. Throughout the 1950s, that was exactly what they did.

The game wardens of the national parks recruited biologists and ecologists, and the latter attributed a 'carrying capacity' to each protected zone – each area was allocated a maximum population density above which eviction was necessary. From that point on, resettlement of local populations increased. And the more the British emptied the parks of their inhabitants, the more tourist-related infrastructures they built within them. The number of visitors trebled, tourism generated millions of dollars and Great Britain was able to repay to the United States the loans advanced to it during the war.[28]

Colonial organizations, international institutions

The same scenario was played out within the other European colonies, under the supervision of the 'new' conservation institutions. Even today, these institutions are reluctant to draw attention to their colonial past. Established in 1956, the IUCN (International Union for the Conservation of Nature) claims to have been created in 1948, under the name of the IUPN (International Union for the Protection of Nature). In reality the Union was already in existence in 1934. At that stage it was known as the IOPN (International Office for the Protection of Nature). And this was simply the new name of the International Office of Documentation and Correlation for the Protection of Nature, founded in 1928.

FFI followed a similar trajectory. Before it became Fauna & Flora International in 1995, the British NGO had existed since 1950 under the name of the Fauna Preservation Society, a title which indeed replaced that of the Society for the Preservation of the Wild Fauna of the Empire, founded in 1903.[29]

The institutions which were founded just after the Second World War also avoided any mention of their colonial origins. Whether it be UNESCO, created in 1945 by the United Nations, or the WWF, founded in 1961 by naturalists and businesspeople, most of the existing conservation agencies had won their spurs in the colonies. From the outset, they were closely involved in the African national parks. They may well have called themselves *international*, but the reality was that they were operating very much within a *colonial* context.

And it is this very story that they want to draw a veil over today. For these institutions acted as reconversion machines for the colonial administrators. In the immediate aftermath of independence, those who remained in the country became 'advisers' for the new African governments. The others became 'consultants' working for international agencies. And all of them continued to claim that in Africa local people were damaging nature. Erosion, deforestation, desertification: these images of environmental change were so widely broadcast that they remained unchallenged at the time of independence. The African leaders adopted them, and, like the colonists before them, they saw the parks as a useful tool with which to control local populations. But the myth was initially perpetuated by those colonial agents subsequently transformed into international experts.[30]

In Kenya, for example, following independence in 1963, many British game wardens were able to keep their jobs. Some forty years later, in 2001, they still remembered that era. At the time, these former wardens recall, they were fighting for 'Pleistocene Africa', in other words, for the continent as it was before *Homo sapiens* and his agricultural methods, 'a Pleistocene Africa which we so enjoyed and sought to preserve but which is gone. It was an impossible dream.'[31] Since Eden did not in fact exist, it could not be preserved. Once colonization came to an end, these men would nevertheless do their utmost to save African nature from the Africans.

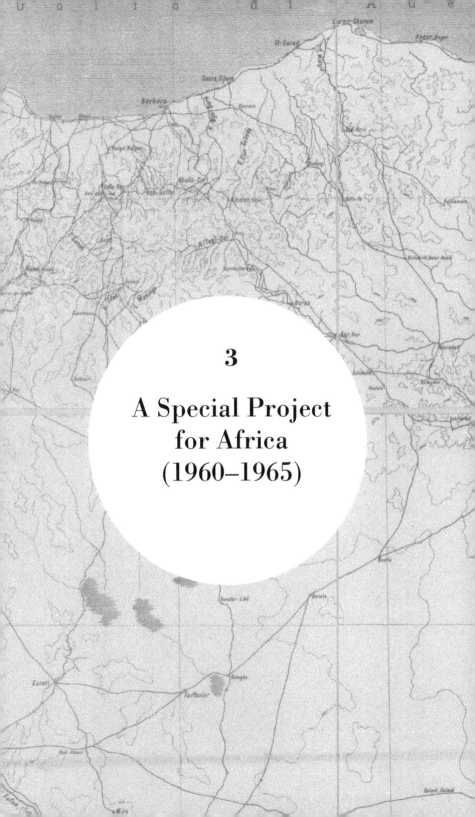

3

A Special Project
for Africa
(1960–1965)

Nairobi, Kenya, April 1965. Leslie Brown is drawing up his mission report. A conservation expert, Brown has just spent three months travelling the length and breadth of Ethiopia. UNESCO has asked him to identify areas which would merit classification as a 'national park', and Brown finds himself particularly impressed by the Simien Mountains.

He even considers them to be the most beautiful natural resource in the country. Beautiful, but terribly threatened. On his return to the Kenyan capital, the British expert is still in a state of shock:

> As we dropped off the Ambaras ridge we came upon a man committing the act of a maniac. At 11,600 feet [...] he was ploughing [...]. Never in twenty-three years in Africa [...] had I ever seen anything to equal this [...]. In progress before my eyes was the process by which the hills of Tigre had been ravaged and reduced from once fair and forested mountains to barren slopes of scree and scrub.[1]

This was only Brown's second visit to Ethiopia, but he was already convinced that the man, this maniac, was responsible for the disappearance of a once dense and extensive forest. Moreover, even before his visit to the Simien, the expatriates he had encountered at Addis Ababa had explained to him that by working the land throughout the whole region, even in the high mountains, the Ethiopians had ended up devastating their forests.

Given that almost half the country lies above altitudes of over 2,400 metres, it is only logical that the Ethiopian mountains should be inhabited and that the land should be cultivated. Yet the myth of deterioration had survived the end of colonization. Worse still, it had even gained strength.

Since the former colonial administrators had taken up roles within the international institutions, they had travelled around from one country to another, crossing each other's paths and passing on their knowledge. Or, rather, their prejudices. Coming from the four corners of Africa, these new experts shared the same conviction: local people represented a threat to nature. And they all shared the same fear. During the colonial period, the Europeans had the power to evict inhabitants from the national parks, or at least to restrict their individual and collective property rights. Since then, however, the western experts were faced with what they described as 'the Africanization of the national parks'. With an independent Africa, they were convinced that, if action were not taken, the future of the parks would be in jeopardy. They needed to act, and to act fast.

Although the African states were no longer under colonial rule, ideas and practices still remained fundamentally colonial. Men like Leslie Brown were the children of an empire and independence was not going to change anything.

Born in India in 1917 to Scottish parents, Brown later moved to Britain to study ornithology and agriculture, and, when war broke out, set off to explore British Africa. In 1940, he entered the Colonial Agricultural Service in Nigeria and then, in 1946, he joined the Department of Agriculture in Kenya.

Ten years later he was made deputy director, and then, in 1962, he was appointed director. But in 1963 Kenya became a sovereign state, and Brown found himself in the position of an unemployed colonial administrator. He took on the role of agricultural adviser for the Kenyan authorities, and established himself as an expert for the international conservation institutions across the whole of East Africa.[2] It was this second role that took him to Ethiopia at the end of 1964. UNESCO had commissioned him to locate potential national parks and to study the state of natural resources in the country.

Brown was not the only expert to be charged with a similar mission. From North Africa to South Africa, all the western wildlife professionals were dedicating themselves to the same task. Under the initiative of Julian Huxley, the international community was in the process of 'evaluating' African wildlife.

Huxley was one of the biologists who, in the early 1930s, had taken part in the African Research Survey, the most important scientific expedition undertaken by Britain across its colonies. A leading figure in the eugenics movement, he became the first director general of UNESCO in 1946, before co-directing the Nature Conservancy, the organization responsible for British national parks. He also continued to work for UNESCO and, in 1960, was sent on a mission to East Africa. On his return in November, he decided the time had come to alert the international community. 'Millions of wild animals have already disappeared from Africa this century. Does the wildlife of the continent now face extinction – threatened by increases in population and the growth of industry in the emergent nations? What, if anything, can be done to safeguard it?'[3]

Huxley's conclusion was categorical. In twenty years' time, African wildlife would have ceased to exist. The 'African Special Project' must prevent this imminent extinction.

The idea first came from the IUCN. At its Seventh General Assembly, held in June 1960 in Warsaw, the IUCN announced that it had obtained the support of two agencies from within the United Nations: UNESCO and the FAO (Food and Agriculture Organization). Thanks to the financial help promised by these two agencies, the IUCN was able to draw up a three-stage programme for the project. Stage 1: meet the new African leaders in order 'to discuss the principles and practices of conservation'. Stage 2: organize an international conference on the conservation of wildlife in Africa, to be held in Arusha, in Tanganyika (now Tanzania). Stage 3: send ecologists into the field 'to help Governments to help themselves to develop their wild life resources'.

The beginnings of the WWF

Gerald Watterson took charge of the first stage. General secretary of the IUCN and the FAO's first regional forestry officer in Africa, Watterson had left Britain for Ghana in November 1960. In the space of two months, he had visited Ivory Coast, Dahomey, Togo, Cameroon, the Central African Republic and Nigeria. Watterson then continued his journey, travelling to the east. He arrived in Khartoum in January 1961 and, at the end of February, he met with the managers of the national parks in Sudan, Ethiopia, Kenya, Tanganyika, Uganda, and both Northern and Southern Rhodesia.

Once this international tour was completed, the IUCN set about strengthening the myth of the African Eden. 'Although several of these countries have not very much left in the way of large, conspicuous wild life areas,' wrote the Union, 'each of them still contains extensive tracts of undeveloped land where the wild flora and fauna is dominant to the tame and where [. . .] the conservation, or in some cases, the reconstruction of wild habitats, could be of great advantage.'[4] Africa, therefore, was tamed but still wild, spoiled but still unspoiled. This was impossible. Irrational. Yet the myth persisted.

These conservation goals were to be achieved during the third stage of the Project. In Ethiopia, for example, following Watterson's visit, the IUCN planned initially to send experts into the country in order to conduct ecological surveys and then to set up the country's first national parks. Except that the Union lacked the necessary funding. The new director of the Nature Conservancy, renowned ornithologist Max Nicholson, was the first to confront this problem directly. Nicholson asked his colleagues to demonstrate some clear thinking. Conservationists needed 'support', he told them, in order 'to share the burdens and provide political muscle'.[5] In other words, they needed more money.

With Huxley's help, Nicholson envisaged setting up an organization which would have a unique purpose, that of fundraising for the IUCN. Both men shared this idea with several of their colleagues, including scientists, business people and penitent butchers in Europe, North America and South Africa. Fourteen men answered their call, and on 29 April 1961 they published the Morges Manifesto, named after the Swiss town where the headquarters of the IUCN was located.

Africa was particularly targeted in the manifesto. It was described as a continent devastated by the savagery of its inhabitants: '[V]ast numbers of fine and harmless wild creatures are losing their lives, or their homes, in an orgy of thoughtless and needless destruction.' Faced with this lack of respect for animal life, the manifesto goes on, funds must be raised with the utmost urgency, experts should be sent into threatened areas and 'local wardens' trained.

The experts in question were adamant that they must have their own budget. This was the key to their influence in the continent. They were in no doubt that the new African states were incapable of carrying on the work of western conservationists. Were they to lose control of the national parks, all their hard work would be in vain – as was evident from the observation that no sooner had colonization ended than an orgy of destruction had begun. Yet they remained hopeful: 'But although the eleventh hour has struck, it is not yet quite too late to think again.'[6] This was their philosophy. Africa had chosen independence; the world fund for wildlife would be their response.

This proposal was discussed in September 1961 in Arusha, Tanganyika. Thanks to subsidies from the FAO, UNESCO and the Fauna Preservation Society, the IUCN was able to bring together 130 experts and high-ranking officials, including forty Africans. This second stage of the Special Project was a success. It was chaired by the socialist prime minister of Tanganyika, Julius Nyerere, and, in his role as spokesman for the African leaders, he assured the western delegates that, in their view, the wild creatures and the landscapes represented 'a source of wonder and inspiration'.

It was a strategic manoeuvre. In order to successfully lead their countries, the continent's new leaders needed the rec-ognition of international institutions, as well as their financial aid. Not surprisingly, they were anxious to appear as reassuring as possible, referring to 'the earnest desire of modern African states to continue and actively expand the efforts already made in the field of wildlife management'.

Julian Huxley was delighted with this declaration. According to him, it was 'a landmark for Africa'.[7] This was an understate-ment. The Arusha conference represented the moment of transition between the end of the colonial era and the begin-ning of independence. The European empires were eager to control African territories and the international conservation institutions were looking for ways to control African wildlife.

And, from then on, they could rely on the subsidies of an independent organization like that proposed by the authors of the Morges Manifesto. On 11 September 1961, just before the conference came to an end, the World Wildlife Fund was created. The WWF would provide financial support for experts who would be working alongside African leaders. This was the third stage of the Project, one which involved sending conservationists to Africa 'to help Governments to help themselves'.

The myth of the lost forest

Ethiopia was one of those governments. On an official visit to France in 1962, the minister of agriculture, Akalework Habtewold, asked UNESCO to help his country create national parks. The United Nations agency accepted and subsequently sent three missions to Ethiopia.[8] At that time, it should be pointed out, international experts were already well established in the country. They had most notably invented the myth of Ethiopia's lost forest, a narrative claiming that in 1900, 40% of the country was covered in forests, as opposed to a mere 4% 'today'.[9]

In present-day Ethiopia, nature policies are still very much under the influence of these figures indicating a drop in national forest cover from 40% in 1900 to 4% 'today'. But when these percentages were mentioned for the first time, 'today' meant 1961. That year, the FAO commissioned one of its experts to draw up a report on the environment in Ethiopia. H.P. Huffnagel produced a report which gave a valuable overview of Ethiopian agriculture. However, when he described the disappearance of forests, he failed to cite a single source.[10]

In reality, the FAO representative had combined two estimates. The figure of 4% came from a report he had come across in Addis Ababa. William Logan, a Canadian forester, had spent time in Ethiopia in 1946 and, on that occasion, he considered that 5% of the country was covered with forest.[11] As for the figure of 40%, Huffnagel had picked it up in the course of a conversation in Addis Ababa with Friedrich von Breitenbach, the founder of Ethiopian forestry studies. In 1961, Von Breitenbach believed that a forest cover of 37% had once existed in an area where today there is only sparse vegetation, even though it is protected by a climate favourable to forest growth. This estimate only applies to the south of the high Ethiopian plateaux, observed, furthermore, just after the rainy season.[12]

These two estimates were totally unconnected and were based purely on simple visual observations. But Huffnagel needed no further convincing. He reduced the first figure from 5% to 4%, while increasing the second from 37% to 40% and then presented them as totally scientific and official data.[13]

James McCann was the first historian to track down the origin of these percentages. His research also took him to southern and western Africa, where he noticed that, here too, colonial beliefs had been elevated to the status of scientific truths in the early 1960s.

In Ghana, for example, in the mid-1930s, the British transformed 20% of the country's wooded areas into national parks. These areas would have apparently been previously covered by a dense primary forest which local farmers had then destroyed, and the government therefore needed to take matters into its own hands before the forest disappeared completely. Seemingly indisputable, this argument was founded on two errors. The first of these was a form of denial since it was not the subsistence economy of the colonized farmers which had increased forest exploitation, but rather the colonial and industrial production of cocoa and palm oil. And, moreover, these forests were in fact not primary, but secondary. This was the second misinterpretation and stemmed this time from ignorance, since most of these forests were man-made. They were produced initially as a result of the fertilization of the savanna areas by local inhabitants, and then by the selective cultivation of cocoa trees and oil palms.[14]

After independence in 1957, Kwame Nkrumah did nothing to correct these errors. The myth of the lost forest had taken too firm a hold for it to simply disappear along with the colonization which had given rise to it in the first place.

On the contrary, the Ghanaian government embraced it, the World Bank reinforced it with the support of various questionable statistics, and the transformation of natural landscapes into parkland continued to be regarded as a solution to this dreamt-up problem. Rather than using their experience to support ecology, and concentrating on the damage caused by the cocoa and palm oil industries, the conservationists clung firmly to their convictions. They focused their attention on the only forest that mattered: the genuine and original 'primary' forest of Africa.

The same situation applied in Ethiopia. No one challenged the incoherence of Huffnagel's report. Yet the results were certainly surprising given that, in 1961, Ethiopia had still not produced a single statistical or aerial study of overall land use across the country, with the first of these only becoming available eight years later. But, for the FAO, the figures supplied by Huffnagel were a perfect illustration of the ecological and demographic crisis in Africa. They published them immediately, with the result that, when UNESCO experts arrived in Addis Ababa in 1963, they were already convinced by this neo-Malthusian narrative. As a result of overpopulation, Ethiopia had lost its forest.

The experts' mission was to help the country develop a policy on nature, but before this had even been fully defined, it was already being shaped by the same false conception, notably that the dense African forest had disappeared. In the case of Ethiopia, to be precise, the forest had diminished from 40% to 4% – a dramatic fall.

The colonists leave; the experts remain

The first of the three missions scheduled by UNESCO took place in September 1963. The Eighth General Assembly of the IUCN was held in Nairobi, Kenya, and five of the delegates attending took the opportunity to travel from there directly into neighbouring Ethiopia. Julian Huxley was in charge of this mission, along with four experts.

Each of these experts was involved in the final stage of the African Special Project. For Théodore Monod, geologist, zoologist and botanist, the task was incidental: his main focus was as head of the Institut français d'Afrique noire (Institute of Black Africa) in Dakar. His three colleagues, on the other hand, had already visited fifteen African countries in the space of a year and a half. Zoologist and former scientific adviser to the British administration in Uganda, Edgar Worthington was then director of the Nature Conservancy in London. Alain Gille, for his part, was trained as an agricultural engineer. He was based in Nairobi, where he was UNESCO's scientific attaché for the African continent. As for the American, Lloyd Swift, a renowned forestry expert and consultant on central and eastern Africa, he was president of the American branch of the WWF.

The five men visited Ethiopia by plane and jeep. They spent only one week in the country, but that was sufficient time for them to conclude that nature was both spectacular and under threat. In the report they submitted to UNESCO, they described 'the remarkable scenery [. . .] outstanding and extraordinary landscape features, a good stock of interesting wild life [. . .] and considerable wild areas of marginal land which deteriorate under cultivation or grazing pressure by domestic stock'.

At first glance, nothing new here: Africa was both natural but spoiled. But this team of conservationists illustrates the transition that was taking place in Africa. Until the end of the 1950s, scientists supported the colonial administrators. The former advised; the latter governed. Independence reshuffled the cards completely. From then on, only the experts were in a position to influence the policies of the African states, and in their own way, they would endeavour to carry on the work of their former superiors. For controlling nature in Africa effectively amounts to managing the territories and peoples of Africa.

The recommendations made by the five conservationists were certainly edifying. They suggested that Ethiopia should create national parks and place them under the supervision of a Council and a Conservation Office. Then, at the end of the report, they added:

> The mission is doubtful whether at the present time there is an appropriate officer within the Ethiopian Government Service to become director of this Conservation Bureau and therefore it is recommended that initially a Director should be sought among the best qualified and most experienced of the Game Wardens or National Park Wardens from other parts of Africa, some of whom are now becoming available.[15]

The message respects the rules of diplomatic decorum. Yet, for all that, it is very clear: the Ethiopians do not have the necessary skills to correctly protect nature. Consequently, they need to turn for help to those western conservationists who are now available – in other words, to the nature professionals made redundant following the independence of the African colonies.

This paternalistic attitude did not prevent the Ethiopian government from following the instructions handed down by the experts. As early as 1964, in the heart of the Mexican business quarter, the brand-new Conservation Department moved into the sixth floor of the Chaï na Buna Building, the premises where the prices of Ethiopian tea (*chai*) and coffee (*buna*) were fixed. A board was also set up to oversee the work of the department. As for the now available experienced director, Ethiopia preferred to wait for the other UNESCO delegations before recruiting for the post.[16]

The second mission took place at the end of 1964. It was led by Major Ian Grimwood, one of the most highly respected figures in the conservation world. After studying biology at Imperial College London, Grimwood served in the Indian imperial army during the war and moved to Rhodesia in 1946. He worked there for ten years in the Game Department, before being promoted to chief game warden of Kenyan national parks in 1960. Grimwood had survived Japanese labour camps and was a hardy individual, capable, according to his colleagues, of crossing the desert with broken ribs. He was also one of the finest field-workers of the IUCN and the Fauna Preservation Society. It was on behalf of the latter organization that, in 1961, he went to the Aden Protectorate in quest of the oryx, an antelope threatened with extinction in the Arabian Peninsula.[17] Operation Oryx was on a considerably larger scale than any previous one. For, at that time, the Fauna Preservation Society professed its fear of one 'danger' above all: that 'when government passed into African hands, many of the existing measures for wildlife [. . .] conservation would not be maintained'.[18]

This fear became real for the major in 1963 when the supporters of Jomo Kenyatta brought an end to British rule in Kenya. Grimwood went on to specialize in consultancy and, in November 1964, he led the new UNESCO mission to Ethiopia. He travelled around the country for two months and subsequently proposed that three national parks should be created: one in the south, in the Omo Valley; one in the east, in the plain of the Awash River; and the last one in the north, in the Simien Mountains.

For the management of these parks, Grimwood advocated firm, colonialist and authoritarian measures. First, he wrote to UNESCO, they must recruit a game warden from amongst 'suitably qualified Wardens from East African countries who have recently been retired as a result of Africanization programmes'. He was also adamant that, in the areas which were to become national parks, it would be necessary 'to extinguish all individual or other human rights'. Finally, in his view, it was indispensable to send Ethiopian personnel for training at the College of African Wildlife Management, the new training centre which the African Wildlife Foundation had just set up in Mweka, Tanzania.[19]

The Tanzanian Foundation was set up to supervise this much-vaunted Africanization of the national parks. A keen safari hunter, Russell E. Train was one of the five founders, all of them from the United States. According to Train, 'The need is desperate to act now.' He explained why: 'With the native races assuming more and more control over the destiny of the African continent, the fate of the wildlife becomes increasingly uncertain.' This is where the Foundation stepped in. Established in 1961, it quickly established the college in Mweka. The goal of the school was to teach 'Africans' the 'international' conservation norms.[20]

Grimwood, too, was afflicted by this same postcolonial anxiety. And his directives would have as much impact on Haile Selassie's government as those issued by Train had had on the Tanzanian government. Ethiopia would recruit a foreigner as chief game warden, it would introduce a restrictive legislation within its parks, and it would send a considerable number of Ethiopian wardens to Mweka. But none of that could happen until the third UNESCO mission had taken place.

Leslie Brown took charge of this mission. He arrived in Kenya in December 1964, a month after Grimwood. He explored Ethiopia for three months and, in April 1965, he came up with recommendations identical to those the major had suggested. Brown proposed that three national parks be set up, and insisted that, before that could happen, existing inhabitants would need to be resettled – from Omo in the south, Awash to the east, and the Simien in the north.

The truth of networked texts

At the same time, in 1965, the experts of the African Special Project were active in all the protected zones of the continent. They were working in Liberia, Guinea, Ivory Coast, Cameroon, Sudan, Kenya, Tanzania, Uganda, Swaziland and South Africa. And whoever they were, wherever they were, these conservationists constantly reiterated the same message: if Africa's wildlife is to be saved, its inhabitants must be prevented from living there.[21]

Decolonization did not lead to any change of paradigm. Nevertheless, with so many new practitioners involved in so many countries, it might have been reasonable to expect that the knowledge handed down from the nineteenth century might meet with some challenge. Yet for over a century, European and North American conservationists had been reiterating the same message: because the 'Africans' exploit their resources in an irrational manner, wildlife in 'Africa' is on the point of disappearing. It would not have been surprising to hear voices raised against the incoherence of such an argument: if wildlife was already so damaged by the middle of the nineteenth century, how come it had not disappeared altogether by now? Since the African farmers were already seen as destructive by the colonists when they first arrived in the country, and have continued to be so ever since, how is it possible that there is still any wildlife left to preserve today?

Inevitably, certain experts must have asked themselves these questions. But the frame of reference was too powerful to be rejected. At the beginning of the 1960s, the subject of conservation had already generated an unprecedented quantity of reports and programmes. These documents had generated a shared vocabulary and shared ways of thinking and of acting. Their content was permeated with the colonial spirit in which they were conceived, yet the very same documents still continued to circulate after independence.

And the same authors were producing even more of them. Their reports travelled from the home countries to the former colonies, from UNESCO to the WWF, from agronomists to foresters. The process continued to intensify until it became self-sustaining. If experts needed to produce a report on Kenya, they simply turned to the one produced by their colleagues in Tanzania, and so on: evidence of the full force of 'networked texts'.[22] Constantly increasing in number, they are distributed more and more widely, and the more they are read and shared, the more acceptable they become. These texts clearly must be telling the truth since they all say the same thing.

And what exactly is their message? How can they manage to make something appear to be true when it is, in reality, merely an incorrect vision of environmental change in Africa? Take Leslie Brown's report, written on his return from Ethiopia and then circulated by UNESCO within conservationist circles:

[The] forest will be gone from Ethiopia in 25 years or so [. . .]. The spread of agriculture is the main threat [. . .]. For many centuries a hard-working people have been destroying their country with relentless energy [. . .]. Most people who visit Ethiopia are inclined to believe that the country was always barren [. . .] and do not realise that many areas have been converted to this condition from luxuriant forest within the last few centuries.

They think that elephants always were scarce in Ethiopia whereas their extermination at the end of the Nineteenth century has been well-documented [. . .]. The destruction of forest which has taken place in Northern Ethiopia over the past several centuries has accelerated in recent years, undoubtedly because of an increasing population and spreading agriculture. [. . .] The remnant patches of cedar-olive forest that are found around churches and monasteries over most of Northern Ethiopia prove that much of the country was once similarly

forested, but they are the only trace that now remains and
much of the country was denuded of its forest cover too long
ago to be remembered by living men.[23]

For the author of the report, and no doubt for its readers,
the argument is entirely rational. It is, however, based on a
dreamt-up image of Africa: of the passage of time which shapes
its history, of the natural environment which gives it its unique
character, and of the people who live there.

First of all, the passage of time. Brown describes a deterioration which is accelerating fast. The disappearance of the forest
and of wildlife began 'many centuries' ago, before spiralling out
of control 'within the last few centuries', declining still further
'at the end of the Nineteenth century' and reaching a peak 'in
recent years'. Without any evidence from scientific data, this
narrative indicates that the colonial myth of the African Eden
is still very much alive: first came the Creation and the long
period in which Africa teemed with bountiful nature, and then
the Fall and the short period in which the Africans destroyed
it.

Next, the natural environment. Brown saw in the patches
of forest in northern Ethiopia proof of the past presence of
'luxuriant forest'. Yet, as is the case in the majority of semi-arid
African environments, these patches of forest are generally
the result of human intervention: agriculture and silviculture
created the conditions needed for trees to grow. This interpre-
tation of the landscape stems from the same mistake as that
made by colonial foresters at the beginning of the twentieth
century. Like them, the international experts believed that the
whole of Africa had once been covered by a primary forest.

Finally, the people. Brown refers to the extermination of
elephants at the end of the nineteenth century. It might be
thought that the British expert had decided to adopt an animal's perspective. After all, the fact that the Africans were
almost as responsible as westerners made no difference to the

elephants. Men had killed them during colonization. But this is neither Brown's argument nor his intent. The expert was proposing that in Ethiopia, game parks should be set up alongside the national parks, where hunting would be regulated rather than banned. For, as he writes in the report, '[I]t is not controlled hunting by capable and conscientious sportsmen that will exterminate Ethiopia's wild life but the indiscriminate slaughter of wild animals by peasants.' It is still a case of the good and the bad hunter, the civilized European and the uncivilized African.

Brown had already had an opportunity to draw up a distressing portrait of the Ethiopian peasantry. He had first visited the Simien area in 1963, on behalf of the IUCN. And on that occasion, he had written to his employers: 'The Ethiopians are without exception the most destructive human beings I have ever seen – utterly feckless and without any regard for the future.'[24] Two years later, it was now UNESCO's turn to learn more about Ethiopia. Thanks to Brown, the agency discovered that in this country, 'a hard-working people have been destroying their country with relentless energy'.

Accounts such as these were appearing all over the continent, thanks to the African Special Project. Where Europeans had cleared the forest, Ethiopians had deforested it. Where the Americans had adapted to the environment, Ghanaians were damaging it. Where westerners were capitalizing on resources, Africans were destroying them. Such analyses were based on racist representations. But the experts were deploying an argument which, on the face of things, appeared so rational that their opinions became facts, and their pronouncements, the truth. This is how, in the aftermath of independence, green colonialism began to take shape. After the racist theories which justified the civilizational burden of the white man, the time was now ripe for green colonialism, born of the declinist theories which legitimized the ecological burden of the western expert, throughout the whole of Africa.

And in Ethiopia, this burden would soon be taken up by John Blower. Leslie Brown recommended him to UNESCO for the post of chief game warden in May 1965, and in September of that year Haile Selassie named Blower as his adviser on wildlife conservation.

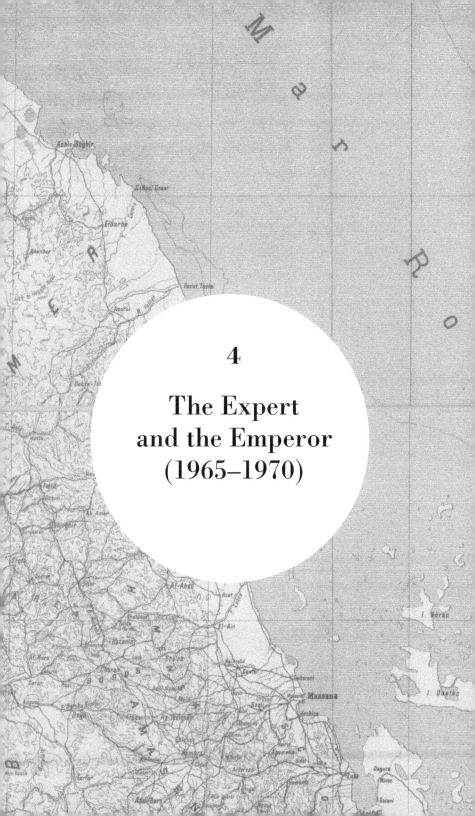

4

The Expert
and the Emperor
(1965–1970)

June 1967, Omo Valley, 600 kilometres south of Addis Ababa. The engine of his 4 × 4 has given up the ghost and for the last three days he has been forced to hunt for his food. He did, however, manage to contact Major Gizaw immediately. The director of the Conservation Authority promised he would send a car as soon as possible, but Blower is still waiting. He will have to go on hunting for a further two days.

Once back in Addis Ababa, Blower is still in a state of rage. All the more so because it has come to his attention that the department's second 4 × 4 could have set off to rescue him on the very day his own vehicle had broken down, if Gizaw had not decided to make use of it to get around the capital, where he had been invited to a number of official receptions. As a result, Blower sends him an incendiary memo: 'Do you wish me to remind you that my being here is on the behalf of UNESCO? [. . .] Can nothing be done to increase the unbelievable inefficiency of this office?'[1]

Gizaw replies the following day. He informs the British expert that he has read the report of his mission to the Omo region. He also informs him that he has taken careful note of his advice about the need to define the boundaries of the new national park. The major adds, however, that he is sorry to have heard that Blower had killed an antelope and some small game. 'The purpose of your trip was not to shoot game for meat,' Gizaw writes, before adding, with increasing irony, 'If you wish to do your own shooting, please obtain appropriate hunting licence like anyone else and shoot if you like in the appropriate areas.' Blower was then punished with a fine, directly deducted from the monthly salary paid to him by the Ethiopian administration.[2]

This episode plunges us into the everyday reality of the conservation world. It demonstrates that, in the period immediately following decolonization, the politics of nature in Africa were postcolonial rather than neo-colonial. Western experts were producing neo-Malthusian analyses which were paternalistic and often racist. But if these discourses exerted a certain amount of influence on the African leaders, it was only because the latter recognized the power of those who had formulated them.

The idea of a virgin nature was an external one, originating from the West. Yet any action always took place internally, within the African territories, deep within the national parks. And in this postcolonial reality, between the expert and the leader, it was a question of domination but also of exploitation and negotiation.

A certain idea of Africa

Blower had served as a soldier in the Royal West African Frontier Force. After the war, he obtained a degree in forestry studies at Edinburgh University and had lived in Africa ever after. He worked in Tanganyika as an assistant conservator of forests, then as a game ranger in the Serengeti national park. He subsequently joined the imperial police service in

Kenya in 1952. The Mau Mau uprising had just erupted, and Great Britain sent him into the Aberdare mountain range in Kenya. Once there, Blower joined the unit responsible for tracking down the Mau Mau rebels. When colonial order had been restored, he returned to his former career in Uganda. He became a game warden and then chief game warden of the country's national parks, until 1962, when independence forced him into redundancy.

This period of inactivity would be of short duration. At that time, the foreign affairs departments of the former colonial powers and the new international institutions were very much on the lookout for men with experience in the field, like Blower. At the end of the 1960s, almost a third of the conservationists from the British Empire were still working in Africa – either in the country where they were living or in another – employed by African governments or the British foreign ministry. And almost half of them were employed by the international organizations working in Africa, such as the World Bank, the FAO or UNESCO. Their status had changed, but not their profession. From Sierra Leone to Malawi, they were still very much conservationists.[3]

In Blower's case, his work would take him to Ethiopia. His fellow countryman Leslie Brown had intervened on his behalf at UNESCO, which in turn recommended him to the Ethiopian conservation department, and, in 1965, Blower arrived in Addis Ababa. He became the first 'Adviser to the Imperial Ethiopian Government on Wildlife Conservation'.

The title represented much more than an honorary position. A month after his arrival, Blower sent a personal note to Haile Selassie. He asked him, without delay, to create the three national parks of the Awash, Omo and Simien. He also urged the emperor to recruit expatriates to manage these parks, to construct safari lodges, introduce wilderness trails, forbid hunting within the park and evict local people.[4] It was Blower who was dictating the terms of the debate.

The British expert was determined to establish close links between conservation and tourism. In January 1966, he himself designed the country's first tourist brochures, and arranged for them to be distributed in the expatriate communities within the capital. The leaflets invited visitors to go on safari. They would see African wildlife such as lions, elephants and buffalo, and a fauna described as typically Ethiopian, like the nyala of the Western plains, or the Walia ibex of the Northern mountains, in the Simien National Park.[5]

According to Blower, Ethiopia should place particular emphasis on the beauty of its scenery. In 1967, he even informed the Conservation Office that the national parks were Africa's only attractions, stating this in no uncertain terms to the director: 'What your department must offer to the visitors [. . .] are National Parks where they can enjoy the magnificent unspoilt scenery of the African plains, mountains, lakes and rivers.'[6] Blower also urged the Ethiopian Tourism Organization to redefine its communication policy, which, in his opinion, focused too much on the country's historic monuments. He was adamant. 'In "selling" Ethiopia to the tourists,' he wrote to the Organization, 'it is critical that the theme must be that Ethiopia has certainly the most spectacular mountain scenery in Africa.'[7]

The Awash, Omo and Simien parks were in the process of being created and Blower therefore felt they should offer visitors an experience of nature in the raw, with fauna, flora and panoramas. But, in his view, in order for that to be achieved, everything still remained to be done. He blamed the Conservation Department for tolerating an 'improper management of the environmental natural resources'. He deplored the presence of local inhabitants and of livestock in these parks, something he regarded as a major problem. Week after week, Blower continued to insist that the department should evict the local people, and then, in the spring of 1966, he suggested to Haile Selassie that he intervene personally.[8] A few months later, the emperor ordered the provincial governors to 'move and resettle' the inhabitants of the Awash, Omo and Simien parks.[9]

Making the colonial dream come true

Amongst all the policies indicating continuity with the colonial era, those relating to nature were very much in the forefront. In Africa, as in Asia, the training centres for future conservationists were still those set up by the Europeans. Trained in the old imperial school, the teachers continued to pass on the same colonial conceptions of nature, and to advocate the same coercive methods to protect it. In Indonesia, Malaysia or India, just as in Gabon, Ivory Coast or Angola, the alliance between power and science continued to hold sway.[10] Continuity was guaranteed by the reproduction of doctrines, of norms and of practices, but also by the presence of international experts like Blower.

The British expert had succeeded in putting the expulsion of local people from the national parks on the Ethiopian political agenda. Unfortunately, much to Blower's disappointment, the operation was slow to get off the ground. In 1969, he criticized General Mebratu, the new director of the Conservation Department, for his failure to end poaching in the Simien National Park.[11] He then urged Abeba Retta, the minister of agriculture, to forbid the free movement of Karrayu pastoralists in the Awash Park. And Blower was especially insistent that police forces should be sent into the Omo region to expel the Surma people who were living within the boundaries of the national park.

The emperor's adviser spelled out the situation to the minister: 'This area totalling some 3,500 square miles [. . .] virtually uninhabited by humans is the richest area in variety and wildlife in the whole of Ethiopia.' But it was under threat. 'Year by year,' Blower continued, 'the number of elephants, buffalo, giraffe, zebra, eland and other animals which exist there are being steadily reduced as a result of pastoralism and systematic illegal hunting by the Surma tribe.'[12]

This Omo Valley does not exist. With a territory of 9,000 square kilometres (the surface area of the Lozère and the Cantal regions of France combined, and with, at that time, a population of 250,000 inhabitants), the Omo cannot be simultaneously farmed by the Surma and yet remain uninhabited. Nor can its fauna be the richest in the country and yet be disappearing at an alarming rate. Moreover, though Blower referred to the disappearance of wildlife, he failed to cite a single figure. How many animals had been killed? How many had survived? The expert failed to provide any clear information. The only evidence cited in his reports is anecdotes, in the form of incidents reported by the park wardens: a hunter caught red-handed or an animal carcass crudely butchered.

Blower, moreover, refused to believe that the Omo Valley was inhabited. David Turton, an American anthropologist, informed him that, in the heart of the park, he had recorded a population of 5,000 inhabitants, all of them Mursi people. But Blower would not hear of it. He himself had visited the region and, he informed Turton, no such 'villages' existed.[13] Yet seminomadic people did indeed live in the Omo region. And that is why animals were hunted there, though not in the way Blower imagined. The Mursi only hunted big game animals on the occasion of certain social rituals – generally those marking the transition from adolescence to adulthood. As for the Surma, their trade in ivory and skins had long since collapsed. At the beginning of the 1920s, the demand of European traders settled in the region had led to the almost total disappearance of big game animals.[14]

Blower's vision of the Omo was more dream than reality. It was a case of nature as it might have been (uninhabited) and nature as it was (inhabited). Thanks to the international experts, the Africa dreamt up by the colonial scientists at the beginning of the twentieth century was finally becoming a reality in the late 1960s.

In this context, Leslie Brown also provided an extremely enlightening portrait of the Omo Valley. In 1969, the ornithologist described it as a region which resembled the most beautiful national parks of East Africa, from Sudan to Mozambique. Brown depicted a landscape that 'has a quality of remoteness; one feels that not only is Man not there in any significant numbers, but that he has never been there'.[15]

It is easy to see how the wide-open landscapes of Africa captivated the western imagination. Such landscapes gave rise to the myth of a virgin and uninhabited continent. But only science can provide a link between myth and reality; or, as Foucault put it, between words and things.[16] In order for nature (the word) to become a park (the thing), scientists have to name it, define it, normalize it. This is precisely what the new experts in Africa were doing, and this was John Blower's role in Ethiopia.

Blower began by drawing up a list of 312 species. The list included animals which it was forbidden to hunt, for example the Walia ibex in the Simien, and others which could be hunted provided a permit was purchased.[17] He then attributed a specific purpose to each of the natural sites to be protected. The parks were places of contemplation, the sanctuaries were dedicated to tourism and to hunting with a scientific objective, and the game reserves were designated for hunting subject to quotas.[18] Finally, Blower set about regulating how these areas were to be used. In the national parks, pending the resettlement of local inhabitants, he proposed fines and prison sentences for anyone caught hunting, and penal sanctions to limit farming, grazing and the cutting down of trees. He wrote to the minister of agriculture explaining that these measures were intended 'to stop the continuing slaughter of wildlife by ignorant and greedy people and farmers'.[19]

The application of these measures would be the first task of the Ethiopian Wildlife Conservation Organization, founded in 1970 to replace the Department of Conservation. Once more, it was John Blower who was behind this professionalization of nature, which, again, corresponded in every respect to the demands of those colonial experts who had preceded him in Ethiopia.

The diaspora of experts

In order to successfully achieve this task, the British expert surrounded himself with a full international team of heritage makers. From 1966, once the three parks to be established in Ethiopia had been identified, Blower sent out job offers to his conservationist colleagues. Agronomists, foresters or park wardens, these were working in Great Britain (for the Nature Conservancy and the Fauna Preservation Society), in Italy (in the forestry department of the FAO), in Switzerland (for the WWF and the IUCN), in the United States (in the Zoology Department at the University of California, Berkeley, and the Department of Fisheries at Michigan State University), in Canada (for the Parks Canada Agency) and in Kenya (at the African Wildlife Foundation and the East African Professional Hunters' Association).[20]

Among the fifteen or so men who responded to the call, three of them became the wardens of the first Ethiopian national parks. Blower sent Peter Hay, a Scot, to the Awash. Seconded from the National Parks Service in the United States, Laurence Guth headed for the Simien Park. And, thanks to his brother Leslie, George Brown, a former district commissioner in Kenya, took charge of the Omo Park.[21] The three men took up their posts in July 1966. They supervised the construction of each park's head office and then recruited Ethiopian guards to patrol the area. Each day, the three of them recorded the flora and fauna, enforced the ban on hunting and attempted to restrict agro-pastoral activities.[22]

If Ethiopia financed part of the work, it was the international conservation institutions that provided the bulk of the budget and technical support. In 1966, the WWF sent a pick-up to the expatriate warden of the Awash Park.[23] In 1967, in the Simien Park, the Swiss Foundation for Alpine Research subsidized Bernhard Nievergelt's first zoological mission.[24] In 1968, the FAO provided logistical support for the construction of a metalled road in the Omo Park.[25] And, thanks to funding from the US Embassy, in 1969, Peace Corps volunteers carried out a number of surveys of flora and fauna in each of the three parks.[26]

This international aid was one of the most powerful tools of the global system which was developing in postcolonial Africa. As political scientists and linguists point out, the discourse which claims to express the universal through the mouth of a universal speaker felt perfectly entitled to overstep the limits of national sovereignty.[27] This was exactly what the international experts were doing.

There are still insufficient data to measure the exact extent of the deployment of these experts in the former imperial territories. Nevertheless, we do know that in the case of British colonies, after the dissolution of the Colonial Service, the Foreign and Commonwealth Office managed to provide the majority of its 25,000 overseas employees with a second career. These were aged between forty and fifty, and most of them were affected by the 'Empire Strikes Back' syndrome, to borrow a term coined by the historian Anthony Kirk-Greene, who studied this postcolonial diaspora in India, Sri Lanka, Tanzania, Sudan and Nigeria. The mentality of these men was so deeply rooted in their colonial experience that they never quite shook off the sense of authority which justified their mission in the tropics.[28]

Certain experts even sought to make Africa pay the price for its independence. Leslie Brown was one of these. In front of an audience of Ethiopian leaders gathered on the campus of Haile Selassie I University, Brown had no hesitation in declaring: 'Funds for the development of wildlife resources are available from outside sources, but they are scarce and they will not be allocated to countries that do not swiftly take steps recommended by impartial experts.'[29]

The international institutions were therefore ready to provide funding only to those countries which were prepared to accept their conception of the continent as once luxuriant and now damaged. As for their impartial experts, for them, protecting Africa was a way of demonstrating their superiority over the African people. Brown took every opportunity to remind the Ethiopian leaders of this. It was imperative that the expatriate wardens should continue to manage their parks, he told them in 1971. These men were there in order to promote the 'changes in ways of life and thought [that] are needed in this country and needed soon'.

Laying down the law in Africa?

Foreigners even went so far as to write Ethiopian laws themselves. In July 1966, the American Donald Paradis, legal adviser to the Ethiopian prime minister, asked Blower to draw up a draft bill on the national parks.[30] Six months later, Blower submitted a first draft to the director of conservation. And he was careful to remind him that UNESCO wanted legislation to be introduced. It was the condition guaranteeing support from the United Nations for the development of the Ethiopian national parks.[31]

With the help of Leslie Brown, Blower spent a year fine-tuning a fully fledged national decree. The two men declared their determination to mitigate the fact that 'this country is at least fifty years behind'. In order to achieve this, they wrote, it would be necessary to 'free national parks from human settlements'.[32] Their text would be taken up word for word by the Wildlife Conservation Order. Published on 5 November 1970 in the official Ethiopian gazette, this law reinforced the restrictive legislation in force in the national parks, subsequently exclusively dedicated to fauna, flora and scenery.[33]

This interference from abroad was not unique to Ethiopia. In French western Africa, for example, the colonial administrators had often had to rein in their coercive ambitions since any attempt to over-restrict local customs incurred the risk of provoking an outpouring of protest. But, in the wake of independence, experts were no longer colonialists. They were merely recommending protective measures to the sovereign states. This position of exteriority therefore allowed them to push through laws which were even more repressive than those of the colonial era. Even in Guinea, under President Sékou Touré, who had voted 'no' to the Franco-African community, a former colonial administrator was to be found at the head of the country's forestry service. R. Rouanet had been head of water and forestry in the mid-1940s, and, at the end of the 1960s, he was behind a law imposing a total ban on all bush fires throughout Guinea, with the effect that, from then on, the offence incurred the death penalty.[34]

All the new sovereign governments maintained a relationship of dependency with the international experts, and with their institutions. In 1963 and 1965, it fell to Ethiopia's ambassador in France to ask for UNESCO's help in choosing his country's future national parks.[35] And four years later, Haile Selassie even went so far as to personally thank the WWF and the FAO for their help in setting up these parks.[36]

But dependence does not mean submission. The emperor had never forgotten that in 1936, when Mussolini invaded Ethiopia, Europe had done nothing to help his country. Nor had Haile Selassie forgotten that he was the leader of the only African country which had never been colonized. He was officially acknowledged as the 225th descendant of the Queen of Sheba and King Solomon, and each of the country's laws carried his seal, that of Conquering Lion of the Tribe of Judah, Elect of God, Emperor of Ethiopia.

This is why in 1965, at the request of UNESCO, Haile Selassie agreed to recruit John Blower. He refused, however, to bestow on him the title of chief warden, or the powers associated with that role. Blower would simply be his 'adviser'.[37] The emperor also reminded all foreign wardens to bear in mind that they were in his country. In order to do this, he waited for the official visit, in the spring of 1969, of Bernhard de Lippe-Biesterfeld, prince of the Netherlands and president of the WWF. On this occasion, the prince asked Haile Selassie to strengthen the power of the expatriates who were in charge of the three national parks, but the emperor esteemed this suggestion to be 'of little relevance'. Then, a few months later, Haile Selassie decided to appoint an Ethiopian warden alongside each expatriate warden, in the Awash, Omo and Simien parks. The message was crystal clear.[38]

Between the international experts and the national leaders, it was as much a matter of domination as of negotiation. In this context, the case of Tanzania is particularly eloquent. In September 1961, during the Arusha conference, the second stage of the African Special Project, Prime Minister Julius Nyerere expressed his desire to continue the work achieved by the British in the country's protected zones. This commitment was by no means feigned. By 1969, Tanzania had quadrupled the budget which had been allocated to the national parks during the colonial era, and the parks were managed in a way which still broadly corresponded to the European notion of African nature.

The management of the parks also echoed targets which were exclusively Tanzanian. Nyerere admitted he was 'personally not very interested in animals'. 'I do not want to spend my holidays watching crocodiles,' he told his fellow citizens. 'Nevertheless [. . .] I believe that after diamonds [. . .] wild animals will provide Tanganyika with its greatest source of income. Thousands of Americans and Europeans have the strange urge to see these animals.' The economic aim of conservation had therefore been amply met.

The strategy was also a political one. During colonization, wherever rebellions erupted, the British created parks in order to evict and then disperse the rebels. The Tanzanian government adopted this method for its own purposes, and Nyerere turned the conservation of the natural landscape and fauna into a pretext to establish villages in rural areas. Creating parks meant displacing former inhabitants, and this meant they could be re-housed in the new villages of socialist Tanzania.[39]

A global game

The conservation world is a cosmopolitan universe. At the end of the 1960s, throughout the entire continent, it was already operating on a predominantly global scale. This involved a three-way relationship between institutions based in Europe, in North America and in Africa. Experts pursued transnational careers, travelling from country to country, depending on the job opportunities. The African nation-states were officially in charge of natural resources, and local populations were affected by the transformation of the area where they lived into national parks. In order to understand how the natural environment was to be protected, the rules of this global game needed to be made clear.[40]

The Law on the Conservation of Ethiopian Wildlife provides a revealing indicator of this tangled web of networks, ideas and actors. The details of how it came to be drawn up provide some insight into the various conflicts involved in the invention of nature.

At the end of the summer of 1968, again thanks to Donald Paradis, the Ethiopian prime minister learned of the decree drawn up by Brown and Blower. In their introduction, the two experts first of all emphasized that it was in 'the national interest to establish National Parks for the enjoyment of the people', and then urged that 'a central administration be created'. Four pages in length, the law, published in 1970 in the Official Gazette (*Negarit Gazeta*), is virtually indistinguishable from the version produced by Blower and Brown, in both substance and form. Moreover, when the EWCO was set up that same year, its first task was to set out a centralized policy for conservation. The imperial authority, however, insisted on imposing two modifications to the introduction written by the two expatriates.

The first addition stated that the parks should be dedicated to the enjoyment of the people, as well as to 'the economic development of Ethiopia'. The financial potential of the natural environment was indeed one of the central preoccupations of the empire. At the end of 1965, Blower had complained about the cost of hunting permits. Ethiopia should be in a position to attract foreigners, he wrote to the vice prime minister: 'It is illogical to impose on them excessively high fees.'[41] The Ethiopian leaders, however, took a somewhat different view. With reference to the creation of the first three national parks in the country at the beginning of 1966, Major Gizaw, director of the Conservation Department, wrote to his superiors that this was an opportunity to 'attract foreign visitors' and therefore a means of 'driving the national economy'.[42]

Haile Selassie himself reiterated this objective in 1967. He asked each minister and department within his administration to demonstrate their involvement in the development of the country's national parks. Their goal – the emperor ordered – must be to 'galvanize the national economy by attracting foreign visitors'.[43] Finally, in 1969, the Ethiopian government introduced its famous two-tier price policy. Even today, in each national park in the country, entrance fees and accommodation costs vary according to where visitors come from, with the price paid by 'foreigners' double that paid by 'nationals'.[44]

This relationship with the outside world was at the heart of the empire's economic strategy. It was also an integral part of its national policy. Take, for example, the second modification to the 1970 law. The Ethiopian legislator took up the recommendation made by Blower and Brown regarding the need to establish a central administration. He then added the phrase 'the necessity to conform to the international criteria'. The latter, according to the law, would guarantee the country 'immeasurable national prestige'. The empire was in fact steering a course between international constraints and nationalist politics.

Like any other country in the world, Ethiopia's power depended in part on its capacity to exist on the international scene. However, like every African state, Ethiopia had not chosen the values of the dominant western model, notably, in this instance, the notion that national parks needed to be emptied of their inhabitants. The empire also needed to keep its promise to UNESCO and the WWF in 1969.[45] The 1970 law defined the inhabitants of the national park as a 'threat', and made provision to remove them.

These international norms acted as a serious constraint. In order to gain acceptance by the outside world, Ethiopia needed to bow to the demands of foreign experts. But if it explicitly referred to these international criteria, it was also with a view to exploiting these more efficiently. As in the other countries of sub-Saharan Africa, Ethiopia's landscapes matched the western heritage categories, and Haile Selassie was determined to take advantage of the fact. The creation of national parks was a way both of gaining recognition for the nation from outside and of reinforcing nationhood within the country itself.

In the Omo Park, for example, the Mursi challenged the power of the central administration. Since 1941, they had even used guns abandoned by the Italians in order to attack government representatives. Financed by UNESCO, the WWF and the United Nations, the park therefore provided Ethiopia with the means it lacked in order to control the Mursi.[46] The same situation was repeated in the Awash Park. After years of clashes with protesters from the semi-nomadic Afar people, the Ethiopian empire used the park as a way of increasing its control within the region. And the inhabitants settled within the Simien Park also frequently clashed with a government they felt was too centralized for their taste. Thanks to the natural environment and to UNESCO, Haile Selassie then had the legitimacy and the funds needed to send his soldiers to plant the national flag in this scrubland region.[47]

Protecting nature, wielding power

Conflict was everywhere. At the highest levels of the admin-istration, the experts and the leaders worked alongside each other, yet without necessarily seeing eye to eye. On the con-trary, John Blower nursed a real aversion to Major Gizaw, the head of the Conservation Department. The British expert felt that he himself should be in charge of the department, and he made this very clear to his Ethiopian counterpart. At the end of February 1969, Blower sent him an impassioned note, one of many such. This time, he railed at 'having to ask repeat-edly each month for my salary to an unbelievably inefficient department'. 'I regret having to write like this,' he declared to Gizaw, 'but when polite requests receive no attention there is no alternative.'[48]

It was a month before the major replied. Gizaw informed Blower of the payment of his salary, and concluded: 'In one of your memos you said that I am anti-British, which is not true. Instead of this if you say I am anti flagrant liar or anti dishonest I would admit [the charge]. [...] I regret having to write this, but when polite approach receives no result there is no other alternative.'[49] The anecdote demonstrates once again that, where nature is concerned, just as in any other area of politics, permanent tensions are rife.

Conflict of this kind occurred throughout the entire country with, on one side, the nationals and, on the other, the foreigners – or *faranji*, as the Ethiopians called them. Blower reproached Ethiopia for being the only country in Africa where resident foreigners were forbidden to hunt; but the government still refused to allow expatriates to hunt anywhere except in the reserves.[50] The authorities also exercised control over visiting foreigners. Tourists complained to those in charge of the national parks, querying the need to be 'followed by an armed man throughout the duration of our safari'. But there was nothing to be done – it was the law. Within the national parks, each group of visitors had to be accompanied by an Ethiopian guard, which also meant they had to pay for all his expenses, including transport, accommodation and food.[51]

If they were on the lowest rung of the ladder in the arena of world conservation, these guards were nevertheless in a position to exercise a very real domination over the inhabitants of the parks. This was evident in the Simien Mountains. In February 1965, the governor of the province founded the Walia Conservation Organization, taking the name from the Walia ibex, a species of ibex endemic in the Simien region. To head the organization, the governor appointed Nadew Woreta, a former imperial official then living in the village of Ambaras. Nadew[52] recruited a team of guards to establish the boundaries of the park, and within only a short space of time, these men were forbidding local inhabitants from hunting small game.

Armed by the state, the guards, however, continued to hunt. Their strategy was identical to that adopted by the Europeans in the colonial era – thanks to the conservation laws, they transformed their neighbours into 'poachers'. From then on, in the Simien Park, the guards alone continued to hunt and to sell the products of their hunting.[53]

They were deprived of their privileges when Laurence Guth took over as head of the park in July 1966. The Africanization of the natural environment had brought the career of colonial administrators to an end and its internationalization had the same effect on Nadew's career. Without being able to claim to be an expert, he subsequently stood as a candidate for the national parliament. And his campaign manifesto succeeded in rallying a considerable number of the Simien inhabitants in that he was calling for the national park project to be abandoned. Powerless to take any action, Guth resigned a year later.

Guth was replaced by Clive Nicol, and he, too, found himself hounded by Nadew's supporters, to the extent that, in May 1969, Nicol wrote to Blower: 'If that shit Nadew gets into Parliament, I see no reason for my staying here. It will demonstrate to the locals that the government is not backing the *farenji*.'[54] But it did give them its backing. The empire formalized the creation of the national park on 31 October 1969, and reiterated its commitment to evicting local populations.[55] At that time, experts and leaders were as much opposed as they were united, and for those living within the park, nature already spelled conflict.

Such was the situation in Ethiopia, an African colonial power ever since the end of the nineteenth century, but the same scenario was repeated in all the former European colonies of western, central and southern Africa. With structures and practices handed down from colonization, the African states remained deeply interventionist. And their hold over local populations continued to rely on the knowledge and the methods of experts, an approach which was also a legacy of the colonial era.[56] This alliance between science and power showed no sign of weakening and would end up locking the parks into a cycle of violence. Working for nature meant exercising power, everywhere, and for everyone.

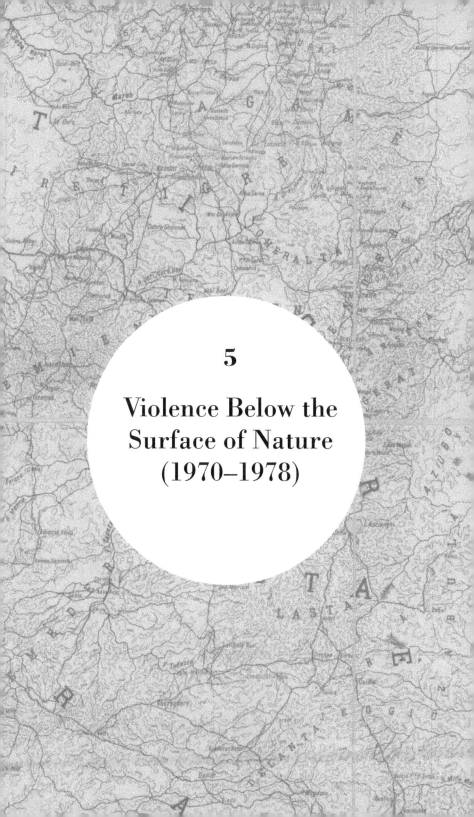

5

Violence Below the
Surface of Nature
(1970–1978)

November 1970, the Ethiopian mountains of the Simien region. Every day, their rifles at the ready, they hunt Walia ibex. The local people hunt not to eat, but to kill. Their sole aim is to slaughter every single ibex. 'There's a certain simplistic logic to it,' acknowledges John Bromley, the new game warden of the Simien Park. '[T]hey figure if they kill off the walia there won't be a park and they won't have to move.'[1]

This is a crucial moment. The inhabitants of Gich would end up being resettled in 2016, but their future is decided here, in this pivotal period in which the colonial era definitively gives way to our own postcolonial period.

The colonized states are now sovereign states and yet the problem of the unrestrained exploitation of raw materials for export to western markets still persists. And if the principle of 'environmental protection' has been replaced by the 'tragedy of the commons', the narrative remains unchanged. Garrett Hardin is the scientist behind this theory. According to this American biologist, the inhabitants of the third world are exhausting resources as a result of their basic and shared agricultural methods, conflicts are already increasing, and if nothing is done, a third world war will break out. On the face of it, nothing has changed since Malthus. Except that Hardin proposes a strategy to deal with the situation: 'mutual coercion, mutually agreed upon'.[2]

The West quickly adopted this doctrine. In 1972, the United Nations organized the first Earth Summit in Stockholm, and rather than questioning the whole notion of development, it established an irrefutable link between the overpopulation of the third world, the depletion of resources and the risk of future conflicts. Then came the oil shock of 1973. The ensuing geopolitical crisis further strengthened the convictions of the international institutions and preventative constraints were subsequently put in place around the ecologies of Africa and Asia. The assumption was that prevention was better than cure.[3]

The problem, for us, is that this global violence is almost imperceptible. It is used all over the world wherever areas are to be naturalized. But those who are responsible for it keep it hidden, very often without even realizing they are doing so. In order to bring it into the open, we need to seek it out in the very places where it is active: at grass-roots level. This chapter sets out therefore to untangle the strands of these ecologies of violence by taking a closer look at daily life within the Simien National Park.

One national park, (too) many actors

A practical approach would be to focus on a face-to-face confrontation between those who live in nature and those who want to transform it into a national park. Except that, to paraphrase Foucault once again, power is not something shared between those who have it and those who do not and who suffer in consequence. Quite the contrary in fact: power circulates and functions.[4]

Clive Nicol's experience bears witness to this. The Canadian had previously worked for the Arctic Research Station. A research engineer, he decided to have a change of scene and, in 1967, applied for the post of game warden in the Simien Park. Laurence Guth had just resigned and John Blower gave Nicol the job. He would remain as game warden in the Simien Park until July 1969, when he in turn would hand in his resignation to the minister of agriculture, who had responsibility for the Conservation Department.

Local people were still living in the park, the construction of the highway to attract tourists had come to a standstill, agro-pastoralism continued to make its mark on the landscape, and, in Nicol's view, the minister was to blame for these failures. He told him so quite openly: 'I am not going to be away from my family to be an ineffective pawn in Ethiopian prestige politics.'

The expatriate also criticized the park managers. 'They are prepared [. . .] to lie about the work that has been done,' he wrote to the minister: 'They only fear the anger of people far superior in rank.' The local guards were the target of even sharper criticism: 'The game guards I am provided with are of the worst imaginable quality. They are illiterate, and are accused of bribery, theft and violence.' Nicol also attacked the former Ethiopian warden: 'Nadew, greatly respected by local people, still encourages the killing of wildlife [. . .], the people of his village appear to be the most active poachers of Walia.' Finally, the Canadian turned his attention to the inhabitants, who were 'obstructive and sometimes hostile. They say that they have Major Gizaw's permission to cut "small trees". [. . .] [T]he Major denies this, and this may very well be untrue, but the people persist in giving us the story, and the story is spread everywhere.'[5]

As soon as nature is involved, power rears its head. The expert drew on his position as representative of international institutions in order to (re)create a version of Eden. The leader used the national park to exert control over the area and to reinforce his prestige. The manager sought to obtain recognition from his superior. The guard took advantage of his status to dominate his neighbour. And the agro-pastoralist attempted to get around the law in order to exploit the land. But these men did not live in isolation from each other. Each of them needed to 'get along' with the others. Whether they liked it or not, the inhabitant of the mountains, the local guard, the regional administrator, the national manager and the international expert were all involved in the same project: that of the national park. And it was this involvement that directly triggered the global violence which we will now analyse step by step.

The myth, the state and the peasant

At the root of the conflict lies the ideology of the international conservation institutions in which the western expert sees it as a duty to save nature which is being destroyed by the African agro-pastoralists. This argument was particularly focused on the village of Gich, at the heart of the Simien National Park. One week after Nicol's resignation, John Blower asked the governor of the province of Simien to resettle the local people. He described them as 'backward and primitive' and 'causing considerable damage'.[6]

The experts dispatched to the park further reinforced the myth. The destruction would continue to happen at an even faster and more intense rate. A former major in the British army, John Bromley replaced Nicol as game warden in November 1969. It took him a mere three months to confirm that 'the remnant forest belts are being destroyed at an increasing rate caused by clearings and ploughing'.[7] The Swiss zoologist J.P. Müller succeeded him in 1972, and he, too, needed no more than a few weeks before writing to the WWF to inform them that overgrazing and farming were causing 'an ever-increasing erosion'.[8] Finally, in 1978, after a number of missions to the park, the Swiss geographer Georg Sprecher described 'exponential' damage. He attributed this to an 'old-fashioned' agro-pastoralism, and to the 'poaching of *Walia*'.[9]

The myth of the lost forest continued to disregard local ecologies, and during this time, the neo-Malthusian narrative of overpopulation far outweighed any actual figures. Nicol recorded 619 inhabitants in Gich in 1969, and Peter Stähli counted 742 in 1974; an increase therefore of 20% over a five-year period.[10] However, in 1976, Hans Hurni, the new park warden, confidently observed: 'The population in the park has increased by about 150 to 250%, i.e. more than doubled over this period and there will not be any change in this population explosion in the future.' Hurni's assessment may indeed have been fallacious, but that did not stop the WWF immediately publishing it in its yearbook, the *Who's Who* of conservationists who were dedicating their lives to saving nature throughout the world.[11]

As for the issue of poaching the Walia, here too the allegations made by the experts provoke a certain scepticism. When he lost his post as warden, Nadew did indeed turn to poaching. How exactly did he do it? Before Guth arrived, Nadew would regularly escort Ethiopian dignitaries and European tourists who had come to hunt in the park – these hunters would then sell the ibex horns to traders from Addis Ababa. When hunting was forbidden in 1966 and Guth took over as his replacement, Nadew was already well placed to become part of the international trade in wild animals. He encouraged his fellow-villagers in Ambaras to hunt (he had lost his title of warden but not his authority), and he sold on the produce of their hunting to traders in the capital city (he had lost his status as a warden but not his contacts). Nadew would abandon this trade at the end of 1969. He entered the national parliament in Addis Ababa and just a few weeks later the imperial authorities identified and then arrested the wild animal dealers.[12]

That said, with the exception of Nadew's former fellow-villagers, this story had absolutely no impact on the lives of those living in the Simien Park. They did not hunt the Walia ibex except in case of famine. There were a number of reasons for this. First, the flesh is not particularly edible. Second, these agro-pastoralists lived in isolated mountains and therefore had no possible contacts which could enable them to participate in an illegal trade in wild animals organized from the capital. Finally, because the ibex is a species of wild goat and consequently lives on rocky cliffs, anyone succeeding in shooting one would then have the task of retrieving an animal potentially weighing up to 125 kilos at an altitude of 4,000 metres.

The image of the 'destructive' 'African' peasant was a western invention and was unquestionably at the origin of the violence. Yet it was not, strictly speaking, the cause of it. In reality, it was the Ethiopian government which implemented the project devised by the experts. In 1969, as a measure to prevent small game hunting, the park authorities created an anti-poaching unit.[13] Then, in 1970, the EWCO banned slash-and-burn agriculture and the cutting of trees.[14] Finally, on 19 January 1972, the imperial authorities proclaimed that the lifestyle of the Simien populations was illegal. The new law was unequivocal: 'No person shall reside, hunt, cultivate, graze cattle or livestock, fell trees, burn vegetation or exploit the natural resources in any manner within a National Park.'[15]

From that moment on, the inhabitants of the Simien Park became outlaws. Farming and pastoralism were punishable by fines and hunting by prison sentences.[16] These sanctions would subsequently depend on the relationships between the local population and the park guards. All originating from the Simien region and many of them former agro-pastoralists, certain guards used their power to exert control over their community. Others, on the contrary, turned a blind eye, through empathy or complicity or for fear of reprisals on themselves or their families. In other words, from the capital down to the village, power was ubiquitous and everybody simply 'accepted it'.

This was equally true for Ethiopians and for tourists and their foreign guides. Ted Shatto was one of the latter. He had left the United States in 1957 to set up the Ethiopian branch of Safaris International Inc. and was a keen businessman. His brochures boasted of Ethiopia's political stability: 'Here we don't have to worry about being kicked out tomorrow, or about nationaliza-tion [. . .], our clients can hunt free of obstructions or worries of any kind.'[17] And for Shatto, this freedom even allowed him to obtain a permit to hunt the Walia.

His compatriot James Mellon had also acquired this special privilege at the beginning of the 1970s. Mellon succeeded in killing an ibex. The animal's limbs were ripped off during its fall down the cliff face, but the hunter's pride remained intact. He had won, he wrote in 1975, a 'supremely covetable prize'. The incident had, moreover, annoyed Yeinatter, one of the guides who had been with him since leaving Addis Ababa. Like Nadew, this man was himself a hunter. So, when Mellon asked him if he knew that the emperor had ordered them not to hunt any more, Yeinatter replied: 'Besides, why are you foreign-ers allowed to shoot the *Walia* when we are not?' To which Mellon retorted: 'Listen, if you keep shooting *Walia* [. . .] you may even be resettled in another part of the country.'[18]

This discrepancy in treatment was the final and most important piece of the puzzle. Mellon and Shatto were the last foreigners to be allowed to hunt in the Simien. The few hundred tourists who visited the national park during the 1970s came to hike and to admire the scenery. But the injustice remained. The inhabitants of the Simien Park had lost their right to farm the land they lived on and this was not the case either for the agro-pastoralists who lived outside the park's borders or for the Ethiopian leaders who criminalized agro-pastoralism, nor for the foreign experts who believed that the Simien area had once been uninhabited and should be restored to that state once again. There was the myth of an Eden and there was the law of the state; there was the injustice which meant being deprived of rights others still possessed; and, then in the end, there was resistance.

Local people first directed their anger against the symbols of the institution which was mistreating them. From 1969, local inhabitants in the Simien regularly patrolled the tourist trails which had been created in the park. They destroyed the boundary markers, signboards and orientational signage put in place by the guards.[19] In response, in order to replace these, the park authorities called on the governor of the province, who sent the soldiers of the imperial army to deal with the local inhabitants.[20]

The mountain people of Simien did not, however, give up, and even went so far as to target the international experts. John Blower himself was kidnapped by *shifta* (bandits) during one of his first missions to survey local fauna.[21] When the Peace Corps subsequently sent Tag Demmett to assist Major Bromley in the Simien Park, they put him firmly on his guard: 'You don't want to get in hot water,' his superior warned him, 'particularly with the local people.'[22] The same anxiety affected the scientists who were working on projects within the park. In the early 1970s, local farmers would some-times shoot at them with rifles.[23] And, in 1976, the EWCO once again referred to the fiercely independent inhabitants. According to the organization, '[T]he people of Simien are suspicious of strangers, especially those who dispense largess and condescension.'[24]

The park guards were not, however, foreigners. They came from the Simien area, but this did not prevent them from being targeted by the local people. On his return from a field trip within the park in 1971, Leslie Brown reported that firearms had been used against park employees. The authorities in the capital were all too aware of the situation. In January 1974, the director of the EWCO expressed his regret that the population showed such little regard for government representatives. He asked the governor of Simien 'to finally put an end to the difficulties which were jeopardizing the park'.[25]

The leader of the province heeded the call and two years later, in 1976, the EWCO was in a position to claim that the risk of attacks on its employees was increasingly unlikely. It did, however, deplore a few one-off attacks, as well as several raids on tourists.[26] And, in 1978, Swiss scientists staying near the village of Gich informed the authorities that the local inhabitants had got wind of their impending expulsion, and were resolved to resist any such attempt.[27]

This fear of being resettled lies at the heart of each act of resistance committed by the local people. Shortly before the official creation of the park in October 1969, some of them attempted to slaughter all the Simien Walia on the grounds that, without any ibex to protect, there would be no park and no further fear of being driven out. On this subject, one year later, the journalist Michael Mok noted the words of one of the Gich villagers: 'It's a strange government that cares more about walia than it does about people.'[28] Cruel and ingenious as it was, this plan to exterminate the animals did not succeed.

The imperial administration subsequently drew up plans for the resettlement of the local people. At the end of 1970, the EWCO proposed giving them cultivable land in the Arsi region, 1,100 kilometres south of the Simien. The park authorities made this plan known to the inhabitants of the park, and a group of about twenty of them was sent to the site of the future relocation. In November 1971, these men visited the land which would be allocated to each family and then returned to their mountains.

They shared their impressions with the other inhabitants of the park and, in December, the agro-pastoralists of Simien flatly refused the offer made to them. They announced to the authorities that nobody wanted to go to a 'country' so far away. The EWCO noted their response but, in January 1972, warned

them that they would have to leave in one year's time, voluntarily or not.[29] Then, at the same moment, on 19 January,
the imperial government decided to ban residence and agro-
pastoralism in the country's three national parks.

UNESCO and the dictator

Only the revolution succeeded in saving the local people from
expulsion. At the end of 1973, the capital was rocked by a
wave of protests organized by students and workers and, in
the spring, this discontent spread into rural areas. Then, in
September 1974, the military committee of the Derg overthrew
Haile Selassie.

Organized by the soldiers of Colonel Mengistu Haile
Mariam, the coup d'état marked the beginning of one of the
most violent periods in contemporary Ethiopian history. It did,
however, offer the inhabitants of the Simien National Park a
short reprieve. The Marxist regime needed the support of the
rural population to consolidate its power. Rather than using
force, they opted instead for a planned resettlement, as the
international institutions had urged. For the Derg had one
objective in particular in their sights and that was to get the
park listed as a UNESCO World Heritage Site.

In a seamless continuation with the policies of the empire,
Mengistu proved himself to be just as welcoming to the outside world as Haile Selassie had been. Blower had left for Nepal
in September 1970, this time in the service of the FAO, and,
thanks to funding from UNESCO and the British Department
for International Development, he was succeeded by three
other experts. The same sixth-floor offices of the Chaï na Buna
Building in Addis Ababa housed first Melvin Bolton[30] and
then Patrick Stracey[31] as advisers to the emperor, and finally,
under the Derg, John Stephenson in the role of adviser to the
EWCO.[32]

With the help of these experts, the WWF, UNESCO and the IUCN were able to send equipment into each of the Ethiopian national parks: radio transmitters, all-terrain vehicles or aircraft. Their employees were also able to continue working on their scientific missions within the parks. In his new role as consultant for the WWF, Leslie Brown made regular visits to the Omo, Awash and Simien parks. The FAO, the Fauna Preservation Society, the Frankfurt Zoological Society and the Peace Corps also took part in this global management of the Ethiopian national parks. They sent technical advisers, biologists and, above all, equipment. Finally, the African Wildlife Foundation provided a number of scholarships to EWCO staff, who were then invited to attend training courses in the Mweka College of African Wildlife Management, in Tanzania.[33]

The empire may indeed have ceased to exist but the Simien Park still maintained strong ties with the conservation world. After recruiting a certain W.E. Lilyestrom for the post of expatriate warden, the EWCO entrusted the management of the park to Swiss academics. The Swiss experts were the first to benefit from funding provided by the IUCN and the WWF, and until 1978, three men successively endeavoured to make sure the ban on hunting, agro-pastoralism and settlement in the Simien Park was respected.

Assisted for a time by Frank Klötzli of the Institute of Geo-Botany at the University of Zurich, J.P. Müller headed the project 'Walia Ibex 753', launched by the WWF in 1972.[34] The geographer Peter Stähli then set about reorganizing the park's anti-poaching unit.[35] And as for Hans Hurni, from 1975 onwards, he became closely involved with the Pro Simien Foundation, financed by the WWF. The Foundation's aim was to heighten awareness of conservation amongst the inhabitants of the Simien Park. According to its president, the Swiss Georg Sprecher, '[W]ithout very deep structural changes in farming and economic methods, which must be related to the attitudes of the population, a long-term change is not possible.' Behind this guarded language, Sprecher had in fact a very specific goal in mind, namely the expulsion of local people.[36]

Whether or not they were convinced of the ecological validity of the operation, the Derg gave it their support. Like the empire before them, the Marxist leaders needed international recognition in order to affirm their authority both worldwide and in the territories which they struggled to control at home. And since the Derg had seized power in 1974, the opposition had gone underground throughout the country. The Simien Mountains were no exception. They had become a powder keg that the regime needed to keep under control, and heritage was increasingly seen as the most efficient tool for this policy.

In 1972, UNESCO launched its new Convention Concerning the Protection of the World Cultural and Natural Heritage. Member states were then invited to submit for consideration any sites within their countries which represented an 'outstanding' interest: that is to say, the Convention clarifies, sites which are 'of outstanding interest and therefore need to be preserved as part of the world heritage of mankind as a whole'.[37] UNESCO added that it would announce the names of the first sites selected for inclusion on the list of 'world heritage sites' in 1978. In the meanwhile, it asked the IUCN to examine the applications for natural heritage sites potentially suitable for future inclusion in the list of world heritage sites.

The Derg suggested that UNESCO should consider including the Awash, Omo and Simien national parks. And Mengistu was determined to satisfy the experts from the IUCN who were responsible for assessing these applications. As early as 1975, the socialist authorities announced that these parks would be set aside for the enjoyment of the Ethiopian people, but also for that of humanity as a whole. Moreover, the Derg toughened the existing regulations. From that point on, the government envisaged the introduction, in all the country's parks, of a minimum one-year prison sentence for anyone killing or capturing an animal. In addition, the legislation announced, fines would now be more dissuasive for anyone caught committing the following offences: clearing forest, cultivating land, grazing livestock, burning vegetation, fishing, collecting honey from a natural hive or disturbing an animal.[38]

The Derg went further still. Three months before UNESCO pronounced its verdict, Mengistu ordered the National Bank of Ethiopia to mint a series of coins commemorating the country's wildlife. Published in the Official Gazette in June 1978, the law indicated that these coins would 'be used to assist the IUCN and WWF in managing programmes to safeguard natural resources and endangered species of wildlife'. The coins were distributed throughout the capital, and each of them featured the image of the Walia ibex, the emblem of Simien, which had attracted western interest for the last fifteen years.[39]

The extravagance of the effort was matched by its reward. In September 1978, the Simien Mountains were amongst the first sites to be placed by UNESCO on its new world heritage list, alongside Yellowstone Park (USA), Nahanni National Park Reserve (Canada) and the Galapagos (Ecuador).[40] The Derg could congratulate themselves on having attained their goal. And they could also bring to an end what felt like too great a confiscation of their national sovereignty. At the end of 1978, Hans Hurni lost his post as head warden in the Simien Park and was replaced by an Ethiopian national.[41]

This decision reflected the motto of the socialist regime: *Ityopia Tekdem* – Ethiopia first. It was also symptomatic of the relationship between the Ethiopian government and the international conservation institutions. Without the expert, the leader did not have complete control over Ethiopian citizens; and without the leader, the expert could not exert total control over African nature. Each needed the other in order to achieve their goal, and the agreement between them was therefore made at the expense of the very people they both needed to subjugate in order to preserve their power: the local inhabitants.

In 1972, Patrick Stracey, the emperor's adviser, was adamant in his communication with the EWCO that every agro-pastoralist in the Simien Park should be relocated. 'This may be summarised in one sentence,' Stracey said: 'all or nothing, by which I mean there should be no distinction drawn between Gich and the other people.'[42] And, in 1973, the EWCO allocated a third of its budget to 'the total removal of any human occupation of the park areas'.[43]

With the Derg in power, it was then the task of John Stephenson to advise Ethiopia. In 1975, the American wrote to the director of the EWCO: '[M]aximum security [. . .] will be achieved only after the extinguishment of all human rights.'[44] And, a few months later, the Derg drew up a national action plan in which they set out 'the ideal solution' for the parks: 'the exclusion of human interference'.[45]

The Marxist military may indeed have succeeded in overthrowing the imperial dignitaries, yet the goal of a natural landscape emptied of its inhabitants still remained. This ideal permeated the life of all the protected zones in Africa. Throughout the entire continent, international experts had replaced the former colonial administrators, yet Eden, the state and violence were still very much present. After the Simien Park in Ethiopia, UNESCO added to its prestigious list the national parks of Zaïre, Tunisia, Tanzania, Senegal, Ivory Coast and Malawi. All over Africa, there were now world heritage sites thanks to which the leaders and the experts would be able to cooperate and unite – on condition that they could remove the inhabitants of those sites.

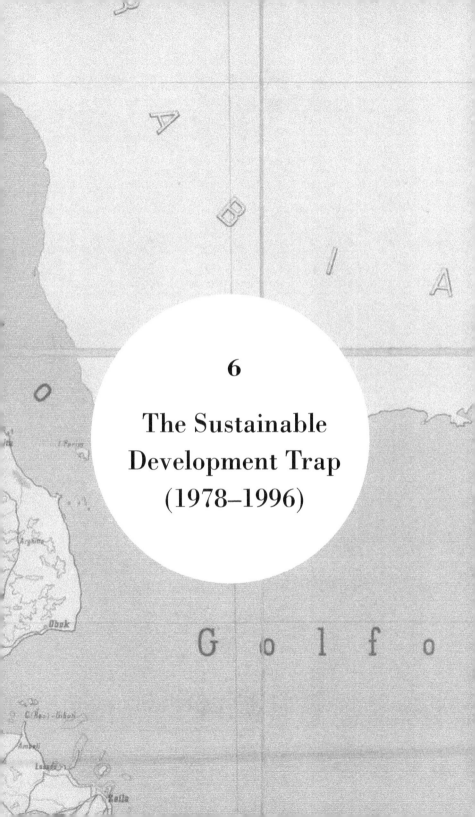

6

The Sustainable Development Trap (1978–1996)

Autumn 1979, Gondar, capital of the northern province of Ethiopia. The soldiers of the Derg emerge from their barracks. A hundred or so of them set off along the road to Simien, 115 kilometres further east. With two days' march to get there, three days in the park and two days to get back, their mission needs to be a rapid one. And it is. A Kalashnikov made in the USSR in one hand, a can of petrol in the other, the soldiers wipe seven villages off the map. The inhabitants of Tirwata, Tiya, Dirni, Muchila, Antola, Agedemya and Amba Ber are driven out and their houses burnt down.

UNESCO hails the success of the operation. On their return from a follow-up mission in the Simien, its employees are full of enthusiasm: 'Some 1200 people have so far been removed [. . .]. In all these areas [. . .], the vegetation come-back is fantastic. Signs of secondary succession in almost all of the formerly cultivated fields are very conspicuous and quite encouraging from the wild-life habitat aspect.'[1] Unfortunately for UNESCO and for Ethiopia, the local people would take advantage of the civil war to return to the park in 1985.

Back to square one. But this time the global discourse was now well rehearsed. The picture presented was still a legacy of the colonial era: Africa is a natural landscape which is being destroyed by the Africans, unwitting victims of their own archaism. The arguments, on the other hand, had changed. The discourse was now so managerial, so slick and polished, that it succeeded in making an eviction look like an apolitical event. And that was the key. Throughout the 1980s, the positive presumption in favour of the protection of nature and wildlife took on such force that the most flagrant injustices could be overlooked even by those implementing them. In Africa, for example, these consisted in the eviction of residents from a national park or the criminalization of those who continued to live there.

Nature remains a national issue

The time had now come for green and global governance. All policies took on a global dimension and, in one way or another, all of them systematically referred to environmental issues. In this new configuration, the question of African ecology joined the ranks of what the international institutions had begun to refer to as the 'major global challenges'. Population health, conflict resolution, the Human Development Index, migration: Africa's problems were now everyone's concern, and would be systematically subsumed under the global management of the environment and its exploitation, conservation or restoration.[2]

This globalization of African nature is very much a reality. But the more prevalent it becomes, the greater the tendency to confuse the global discourse with the national realities. This is where the problem lies. On the one side there is the discursive context created by the international institutions and within which they act – a great single entity named 'Africa' – and, on the other, there is the political framework within which nature is shaped: the African governments. In order to distinguish between the two, the first step must therefore be to acknowledge that, unlike the narrative which underlies them, global policies on nature do not come out of nowhere. They always have a specific context.

In South Africa, during the 1980s, apartheid and nature were indissociable. Within the national parks, the battle with the 'African demographic danger' was used as justification for the eviction of local people, and, throughout the country as a whole, for spatial segregation.[3] In Tanzania, where 25% of land had been transformed into nature reserves, the socialist regime turned the ecological argument into justification for ever more centralized land tenure policies. Thanks to nature, the state was able to infiltrate villages, down to the lowest level of the nation's territorial fabric.[4] In the vast expanses of Zaïre, the creation of national parks near the country's eastern borders served even more simply, and more violently, to subjugate those territories which had rejected Mobutu's authority.[5] And in Mengistu's Ethiopia, transforming natural landscapes into national parks was one of the tools used by the Derg to crush the opposition.

The Ethiopian case shows the extent to which protecting nature is first and foremost a matter of politics. The Marxist-Leninist leaders abolished the land tenure system in 1975. They nationalized the means of production, launched a campaign to collectivize land in the course of which tens of thousands of farmers were displaced, and, very quickly, their opponents took up arms and then went underground. This resistance explains why the Derg were so quick to remove the management of the Simien Park from the Swiss. The regime was keen to use the park to demonstrate its independence vis-à-vis the outside world, but it was also determined to implement the agrarian revolution on its own terms.[6]

In order to carry out this task successfully, in the new province of Gondar, governor Melaku Tefera hunted down opponents with unprecedented violence. In the Simien region, transformed at that time into a hotbed of resistance, directives issued by UNESCO made his task easier. In 1978, the organization had once again recommended the resettlement of local people, and as a result, in 1979, Melaku's soldiers destroyed the seven villages within the Simien Park. Thanks to the insistence of international experts, half the population of the park (1,200 inhabitants) were expelled and resettled in the new socialist villages created by the Derg.[7] Mengistu drew inspiration in this case from his Tanzanian counterpart, Julius Nyerere.

UNESCO subsequently sent two of its experts to Ethiopia. These were the agronomist Charles Rossetti and an ecologist, Ermias Bekele. The two men witnessed the extent of the Derg's determination. The authorities had been planning the resettlement of the village of Gich since 1982. It was, according to them, the only way of combating 'the continued devastation and overgrazing that is taking place in the area'.[8] Then, in 1983, Mulugeta Ayele, the director of the EWCO, set out plans to resettle all those living within the park. He announced his intention to the two UNESCO representatives in Addis Ababa. Ethiopia, he told them, was determined 'to enhance the international values and responsibilities for the conservation and development of the park to make it truly a world heritage site'.[9]

Only the upsurge in opposition prevented the Derg from achieving their goal. In the south of the country, the Oromo Liberation Front was attracting growing numbers of supporters. In eastern Ethiopia, armed groups were receiving aid from Somalia under the leadership of Siad Barre. In the north of the country, the Eritrean People's Liberation Front was daily gaining ground.[10] These were joined by the rebels of the Tigray People's Liberation Front, and in 1984, these two secessionist movements established their headquarters in the Simien Mountains.

The national park then became the epicentre of the 'red terror' that the Derg had agreed to inflict on their enemies.

The Simien guards were enlisted to fight the insurgents, and the regular soldiers of the Derg took action against any local inhabitants who were supporting them.[11] Just outside the village of Chenek, at an altitude of 3,500 metres, soldiers of the Derg threw those they suspected of collusion with the rebels over a cliff in order to save on ammunition. This practice gave the place its nickname: the cliff of the dead. Such was life in a national park listed by UNESCO. Under the influence of the globalization of heritage, the African states exploited the standards of green and global governance in order to impose the violence of their regime.

Nature remains a colonial idea

It is worth pointing out that the international institutions quickly came to terms with such brutality. In Ethiopia, the rebellion and its repression simply obliged the experts to keep away from the parks themselves. UNESCO continued to train guards for the Ethiopian parks in Addis Ababa,[12] and at the request of the Derg, the organization agreed to prepare the very first management plan for the Simien Park. With a first phase involving consultations between the EWCO, the IUCN and the universities of Bern and of Zurich, the full plan was drafted by the geographer Hans Hurni in 1986. Employed on this occasion by UNESCO, the former warden of the Simien Park planned to include 'conservation' and 'integrated development' within the plan.

The plan was printed in Switzerland by UNESCO, and then distributed in Ethiopia in the name of the EWCO. In it, Hurni began by outlining the existing situation within the country. No localized study was carried out, no verifiable figures were provided. Just three terse conclusions. Humans have destroyed the forest: 'Almost 40% of the Ethiopian highlands were once covered by dense forests. Today, this figure is estimated to be 2.8%, showing the extent of deforestation in the past 2000 years.' Agro-pastoralists have caused wild animals to disappear: 'Wildlife is rare in the Region due to the high rate of deforestation and due to annual burning of the grassland.' As for overpopulation, the situation would only get worse: 'Vast areas have already been abandoned, and due to population pressure even more areas will have to be left out in future.'

The prognosis was just as catastrophic in the Simien Park, there, too, without reference to any genuine study. The park, Hurni wrote, provides 'a "back to nature" feeling'. But, in his view, humans were jeopardizing the future of this nature: '[C]enturies of mis-use have led to [. . .] a reduction of forests from formerly 80% of the Simien to about 10% at present.' Nor was that all. According to Hurni, '[H]uman occupancy and overutilization of natural resources for almost 2,000 years [. . .] lead to deforestation, soil degradation, destruction of wildlife habitats and reduction of wildlife.'[13]

What could be said in response to such neo-Malthusian analyses? Once again, on the surface, there was nothing new here. Too many people who had ended up destroying the space in which they lived, destructive agro-pastoral methods, a natural world which still existed but which was nevertheless in decline: the narrative ticked all the boxes of the myth of the African Eden.

But it also echoed the new discourse which was being developed by western conservationists. Bernhard Grzimek was the most influential of these in East Africa. A German zoologist and film director and an ardent defender of nature since the 1950s, he sang the praises of the work carried out in the African national parks which was then being duly rewarded by UNESCO. In their 'gardens of Eden', wrote Grzimek, the African states did not hesitate to relocate entire villages, 'something that was never proposed under European colonial rule, let alone done: to be willing to evacuate people to make room for animals'.[14]

This was new. The arguments were still those inherited from colonization: because Africans had been destroying nature for 2,000 years, protecting it was a matter of urgency. In other words, the agro-pastoralists must be sanctioned and, eventually, relocated. But this time, the conservationist elites were claiming that the idea came from the African leaders. Any expulsions were on the basis of their initiative and the international institutions would simply be supporting them in their struggle. The undertaking would no longer have any connection with colonialism, either in terms of its conception or in terms of its implementation.

The norms had indeed changed. Since the early 1980s, the protection of nature was supposed to improve the lives of local people. It was from this perspective that in Ethiopia, in line with what was to become common practice, UNESCO proposed moving the local people from the 'core zone' of the Simien Park and relocating them on the other side of the park borders, in a 'buffer zone'. There, 'development' programmes would provide them with a 'better life', according to the new terminology deployed within the conservation world.[15]

Between this type of discourse and the implementation of such strategies in the field, the gulf could hardly be wider. In Ethiopia, when the management plan for the Simien Park was published in 1986, local people who had been evicted had already returned and had rebuilt their villages within the park.[16] The Eritrean and Tigray rebels had held the mountains since 1985, and the legislation of the park had effectively been suspended as a result. The Simien area at that time provided 'a sense of peace and pastoral prosperity', as one visitor recalled.[17] Paradoxically, the outbreak of war had triggered a return to normal life for the agro-pastoralists. This was why, in 1991, when the Derg lost power, local people nurtured the hope that they would no longer be troubled by the national park. They destroyed the camps used by the park guards and, once again, set about destroying the Walia ibex. Their argument was the same as in 1969: without the ibex to attract the attention of UNESCO and tourists, the state would abandon the park.[18]

Their attempts met with failure once again. In May 1991, Tigray, Amhara and Oromo rebels overthrew the Derg and replaced them with their own coalition: the Ethiopian People's Revolutionary Democratic Front. American Jesse Hillman, adviser to the EWCO for the previous ten years, seized the opportunity to return to the park. He arrived at the foot of the Simien Mountains in October and, to his great surprise, found his way barred by armed men. These, it turned out, were agro-pastoralists and they made it clear that, regardless of whether he had been sent from Addis Ababa, if he wished to go into their mountains, he would first of all have to hand over some money.[19]

Control over the area by those who lived there would not, however, last for more than a few months. Where the empire and the Derg had subjected the local people to a fortress conservation model, the Federal Democratic Republic of Ethiopia would instead impose a community-based conservation. This paradigm is the new norm in the worldwide management of nature. It does not change the vision of nature in Africa in any way. Yet, from Zanzibar to South Africa, it everywhere raises the same question: who owns Eden?[20]

A new way of seeing Africa?

The community-based approach goes hand in hand with that of sustainable development. The origin of the concept dates back to 1980, when the United Nations asked the IUCN to formulate a leadership plan which reconciled protection of nature and globalization of the economy. With this in mind, twenty years after the Africa Special Project, the IUCN once again brought together conservationists from UNESCO and the WWF and developmentalists from the FAO, the United

Nations agency for food and agriculture. And this time, the experts devised a World Conservation Strategy. They were unanimous that the international community should, from that moment onwards, work towards a single and shared goal, that of 'sustainable development through the conservation of living resources'.[21]

This statement of intent was more sharply defined after 1983. Under the presidency of the Norwegian Gro Harlem Brundtland, a UN Commission on Environment and Development brought together a hundred or so national, international and non-governmental institutions. Together, several thousand experts explored how to reconcile food safety and the depletion of resources, ecological risk and industrial pollution, economic growth and social equity. Their task was completed in 1987. Under the title *Our Common Future*, the Brundtland Report defined the concept of 'sustainable development'.[22] The principle was intended to be unambiguous: it sought to meet the needs of the present without compromising those of future generations. It was also ethical. For Brundtland, 'It is both futile and indeed an insult to the poor to tell them that they must remain in poverty to protect the environment.'[23]

The second Earth Summit therefore marked the official opening of the era of sustainable development: our own. A hundred or so states met in Rio in June 1992 in order to sign the Convention on Biological Diversity. They undertook to promote the conservation of biodiversity, the sustainable use of biological resources and the equitable sharing of any benefits arising from these.[24] The international community also declared that in natural parks, in particular in Africa, this conservation would be 'community-based'. Ecosystems would be seen as dynamic, rather than static. Nature would be perceived as something shaped by humans, rather than damaged by them. And instead of finding themselves excluded, local people would be involved in nature and conservation.[25]

It would be difficult not to succumb to such a discourse. And with good reason, given that its primary, even unique, function is to reassure. In the face of industrial, ecological and climatic catastrophes, the challenge of the Brundtland Report and the Rio Summit was to reconcile the irreconcilable, in other words, the capitalist exploitation of resources and their protection for the whole community. Gilbert Rist perfectly summed up the philosophy of the rhetorical stratagem represented by sustainable development: the bait may indeed be alluring, but there should be no mistake: what the world wants to be sustained is development, and not the capacity of the environment to tolerate its impact.[26]

The discourse is, moreover, all the more artificial in that in Africa, it had little or no impact on the management of nature.

First, there was the hierarchy of knowledge. From the beginning of the 1980s, the NGOs and the international conservation institutions had claimed to take account of 'local knowledge'. In reality, such knowledge was only ever regarded as complementary.[27] Only official data really counted, and this was always taken from reports produced and exchanged by experts. Such reports continued to advocate continent-wide theories based on local surveys and figures which were incomplete or incorrect, and the experts systematically described African ecologies as being under threat from those who were living in them.[28]

Then there was the enduring nature of existing practices. If the approach of the fortress method of conservation had theoretically been abandoned, expulsions still remained common practice in the African national parks. Such relocations now needed to serve the community, transported from a core zone dedicated to nature to a buffer zone dedicated to development.[29] But the same pernicious effects still persisted.

When agro-pastoralists were resettled in a buffer zone, they arrived with their livestock, and the operation resulted in an influx of cattle. As a result, the market price dropped and, inevitably, people found themselves getting poorer. In the core zones, where local people were authorized to remain, the condition for doing so was a reduction in agricultural activity. In such cases, the process led to an intensification of the pastoral economy since this became the only way of compensating for the inability to work in the fields. As a result, the land was overgrazed by cattle and unable to regenerate, and, inevitably, local people ended up losing their means of subsistence. In Africa, for those living within a national park, conservation always went hand in hand with poverty.[30]

And, finally, there was the myth. Throughout the western world, ecological deterioration now seemed irreversible. Oppressed by the drama playing out on their own doorsteps, the inhabitants of the northern hemisphere found themselves dreaming of an Africa transformed into a wildlife sanctuary. More than ever before, they needed to see it as a continent of refuge where it was possible to escape from the technology, industry and pollution which was undermining the rest of the planet.

Various forms of media helped to spread such concepts. With documentaries like *Life on Earth*, a programme created by David Attenborough and the BBC, television transported its audiences from mountains to deserts, from forests to idyllic shores, and all without really describing the places and the societies filmed. Instead, there was simply a vast 'Africa' which was natural and homogeneous.[31] Meanwhile nature magazines like *National Geographic* continued to portray a continent which was intrinsically wild, where 'tribes' still lived far from civilization, in the heart of an 'African nature' which was, of course, threatened, but which had nevertheless managed to avoid development.[32]

The cinema, too, reinforced this image of an Eden-like Africa. Thanks to Disney, for example, in 1994, more than one hundred million children and adults discovered the story of *The Lion King*. Very few of them realized that the film was inspired by *Jungle Emperor Leo*, an animated film shown on television in the early 1960s, and directly inspired by the colonial era. On the other hand, many spectators retained the image of a green planet, where enlightened autocrats (the lions) prevented destructive creatures (the hyenas) from burning the savannas.

Touching as it is, the tale reflects with disturbing clarity the actions of western conservationists in Africa, for their part also acting like deposed leaders. Like the colonial administrators before them, they were convinced that they were the only ones capable of understanding nature and the circle of life. And, like their predecessors, the international experts saw themselves entrusted with a duty: that of saving planet Africa before its inhabitants managed to destroy it.[33]

A new way of seeing the Africans

With colonization now a thing of the past, these conservationists no longer had a monopoly over African nature. Their discourse nevertheless remained resolutely hegemonic, as is evident from the standardization of conservation programmes. In Ethiopia, between 1985 and 1990, the Derg were responsible for the planting of 300,000 hectares of forest and the construction of 500,000 kilometres of agricultural terraces. This programme, as was by then the norm, was co-financed by NGOs and by the United Nations 'Food-for-Work' programme. The problem was that these programmes failed to address the problems faced by the peasant farmers they were supposed to benefit, notably animal diseases, a semi-arid climate, lack of arable land and the rigidity of land tenure systems.

The result was therefore catastrophic. While the construction of terraces reduced agricultural production, forests planted in a conservation zone led to a damaging overconcentration of cattle just outside the limits of the protected area. Angry at finding their real problems ignored, the agro-pastoralists immediately set about destroying the reforested enclosures.

The same failures encountered in Ethiopia were repeated in Nigeria, Namibia, Mozambique and Sudan. In all of these areas it was the same story. *In the past*, a sparsely populated Africa rich in resources; *today*, an overpopulated continent where people needed help to restore the balance they themselves had disturbed. And in all of them, the results were the same. Born out of an endless neo-Malthusian logic, these programmes failed to help the very people for whom they were intended. They simply suited those responsible for their implementation.

In the first place, they allowed Europe and the United States to finance the 'Food-for-Work' programme. Thanks to this, the two superpowers offloaded any surplus from their own agricultural production and, under the pretext of humanitarian aid, were in a position to fix world wheat prices to their own advantage. Second, such programmes corresponded to the aims of NGOs, keen to help Africans with rapid and visible results. Finally, they bolstered the careers of western experts and African leaders. The former controlled nature, and the latter the local population. Given that this was the only way of obtaining the food they lacked, local people were all willing to work in the interests of conservation, and for the state.[34]

Locked in the throes of war, the Simien Park did not get involved in this type of programme until March 1990. At that point, Ethiopia asked the IUCN for help in defining a National Strategy for Conservation, and the director of the Union went in person to Addis Ababa. 'It is no longer the time for interference,' Martin Holdgate announced to the Ethiopian leaders, adding: 'My colleagues from IUCN and your partners from international and bilateral organizations are here to help. But our role is subordinate to yours.' EWCO director Teshome Ashine expressed approval. He went as far as to condemn the 'present mediocre system' hitherto, according to him, acting 'as a "fillip" to conscience, to Western wildlife conservation societies and Western animal lovers, but to the exclusion of the needs of the Ethiopian general public, striving to survive'.[35]

This type of discourse clearly echoed the Brundtland Report. As did the results ... With the Simien now accessible once more, Ethiopia called upon the international community to assess the state of the Simien Park and, very quickly, all the institutions involved in the conservation of natural resources in Africa gathered in the area. Together they would lay down the foundations for the new community-based conservation programme.

An initial mission took place at the end of 1991. Jesse Hillman, adviser to the EWCO, represented the Wildlife Conservation Society, an extremely influential American organization. The American visited the park and observed the damage caused by the war. He suggested that the EWCO urgently rebuild the guards' camps within the Simien.[36]

Then, in 1993, a second mission was jointly organized by the United Nations Sudano-Sahelian Office (UNSO) and the United Nations Development Programme (UNDP). The man in charge of the operation was David Crabtree. After flying over the Simien Park in a helicopter, he recommended the reconstruction of infrastructures destroyed by the war, the rehabilitation of wildlife and nature under threat from local people, and the resettlement of the latter.[37] He needed no more than a single day to assess conditions in the park and to decide on the fate of its inhabitants.

Finally, in the spring of 1994, it was the turn of the United Nations Capital Development Fund (UNCDF) to organize a third and final mission. To do this, the organization turned to Farm Africa, a British NGO based in East Africa. Over the course of a week, the mission, led by anthropologist Richard Hogg, and also including a forester, an agronomist and two Ethiopian development planners, flew over the Simien area. They also spoke to the inhabitants of six villages within the park.

The experts submitted their report to the UNCDF and the EWCO in May. The report highlighted two problems: 'defor- estation' and the local people's 'considerable suspicion and fear of resettlement'. As a result, the two organizations announced their opposition to the resettlement recommended by the previous mission. Occupancy of the park was a reality and the solution, according to these experts, was 'to introduce in Ethiopia the same community approach used in East Africa'. Farm Africa was particularly adamant on this point. Working with local people was the only possible way of achieving 'sus- tainable rural development within the Park'.

Yet none of these observations prevented the NGO from recommending . . . the expulsion of the local people. 'The plan of action recognises that there may at some future date be a need to introduce a phased re-settlement programme,' wrote the experts at the end of their report. 'However,' they added, 'there is first a need to win the confidence of local people and to show them, in practical ways, the potential benefits the Park can bring to them and their communities.'[38]

From that point on, this was the favoured ethical code throughout protected zones in the tropics, from West Africa to South-East Asia.[39] If the community was now seen as the solution, it nevertheless continued to be the problem: peas- ant farmers were endangering nature, and in order for it to be saved, they would have to leave. Nothing had changed. The arguments remained paternalistic, declinist and impli- citly racist. Except that the resettlement of local people was now supposed to be a way of helping them. By leaving their natural environment, the local farmers would end up saving themselves.

New ethic, old ways

It was in this context that the Simien Park once again opened its gates to visitors. In 1994, 340 tourists, including nineteen Ethiopians, visited the park. The WWF subsequently set up a 'trust fund' devoted to the Ethiopian parks, and, thanks to subsidies from the four agencies of the United Nations (UNESCO, the FAO, the UNDP and the UNCDF), the park managers were able to double the number of staff employed on the ground. Their first task was to reconstruct what the war had destroyed, notably the camps which enabled guards to supervise the park, and the hiking trail which allowed tourists to explore it.[40]

The work to be carried out in the Simien was finally set out in the course of two workshops organized by the EWCO, Farm Africa, the United Nations, the University of Bern and the British and Austrian embassies. The first workshop was held in Gondar in February 1995 and involved about twenty people, including some of those living in the park. A farmer from the village of Adi Arkai voiced his discontent: 'He asked what was the use of democracy if what his community asked for was not heard,' recorded the minutes taken during the meeting. A local deputy took up the baton: '[I]nhabitants do not need only studies and workshops [. . .]. There were big problems 20 years ago. They are still here today. The people need transport, health, education, businesses and roads.'

The Ethiopian leaders and the international experts were reassuring. They promised that, from then on, conservation would involve local decision-makers and local people. Agriculture would be improved in a buffer zone where residents would be resettled outside of the park. They would be offered jobs as guides, porters and cooks. And their resettlement would be 'voluntary'.[41] This was the new ethical code. Local people would not strictly speaking be evicted, since they would have chosen to leave 'voluntarily'.

The second workshop took place in Addis Ababa in mid-May 1995 – a decisive moment for the leaders of the Ethiopian Democratic Front. If the Constituent Assembly were to validate the Constitution they had prepared for the new Federal Republic of Ethiopia, the leaders of the Front would officially take control of the country. The vote was due to take place a few days later and they needed to be able to prove to the Assembly that they could put the country back onto the international stage. It was hardly surprising therefore that they, like the empire and the Derg before them, should adhere closely to the norms currently in force within the conservation world. The workshop included many delegates from the United Nations and, in the presence of these representatives, the Ethiopians voiced their continued commitment to protect the Simien Park from deforestation, overgrazing, overexploitation and erosion. They also took the opportunity to make the solemn promise that their work would be in keeping with the new conservation watchword: 'Parks for People'.[42]

As for the western conservationists, they, too, continued to act along exactly the same lines as their predecessors from the colonial school. It was they who singled out for blame the vicious circle of deforestation–overgrazing–erosion. It was they who identified the resettlement of local residents as a means of achieving an African ideal in terms of fauna–flora–panorama. And it was they, too, who recommended that UNESCO should downgrade the Simien Park from its list of world heritage sites onto its List of World Heritage in Danger.

In June 1996, on the basis of their long experience in the Simien Park, the geographer Hans Hurni and the zoologist Bernhard Nievergelt were commissioned by UNESCO to undertake a 'technical mission' within Ethiopia. The two Swiss academics arrived in Addis Ababa on the evening of Saturday, 2 November. Over the course of Sunday, Monday and Tuesday, they took part in nine meetings with Ethiopian leaders and members of UNESCO, the IUCN and the United Nations.

Then, that same evening, they flew to Bahir Dar, the capital of the Amhara region where the Simien Park is located. On the Wednesday and Thursday of that week, Hurni and Nievergelt hosted a workshop bringing together administrators from the region and from the park, and then, on the Friday, they returned to Addis Ababa. The following day, they attended a further two meetings, one with an Ethiopian rural planning expert and the other with the Swiss ambassador in Ethiopia. The two consultants left for Switzerland in the evening, at the end of a single week's work.

They did not go into the park. Neither of them undertook any surveys in order to assess the state of fauna, flora and soil within the Simien. Yet in spite of that, the report they sent to UNESCO was no less sententious in tone. 'Serious and specific danger exists from the intensifying human use of over 80% of the Park area, including degradation processes of fauna, flora, and natural resources,' wrote Hurni and Nievergelt. They announced that they were 'convinced that the site should be included in the List of World Heritage in Danger'. According to them, such a measure would encourage Ethiopia to finance the two programmes needed to guarantee the successful management of the park: raising awareness amongst the local people and then their voluntary resettlement.[43]

UNESCO took note. The World Heritage Committee followed the recommendations made by the experts and, on 7 December, the penalty was imposed. The Simien Park was downgraded to the List of World Heritage in Danger, and UNESCO ordered Ethiopia to introduce 'effective' community conservation there.[44]

The same fate would befall the parks in Guinea, Niger, the Central African Republic and Congo-Kinshasa. In each case, the procedure was exactly the same. The international experts were working towards a uniform global governance. Their principles were moral ones (they were fighting poverty, hunger and disease) and their norms were supposedly ethical (development had to be sustainable, community-based and participatory).[45] Yet their professional practice remained marked by their ignorance of local realities, combined with a conviction that Africans have no place in nature. In the Simien Park, as in so many other parks across the continent, local people therefore made their definitive entry onto the globalization scene against the background of this deeply contradictory situation: give nature to the people; prevent the people from living in it.

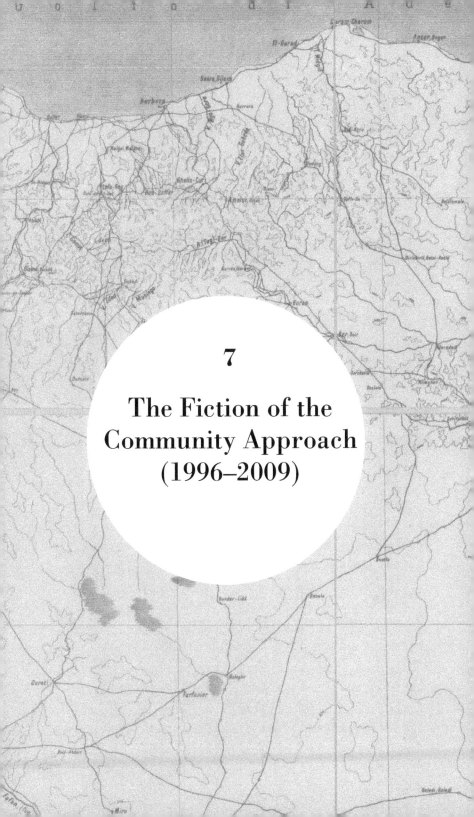

7

The Fiction of the Community Approach (1996–2009)

Addis Ababa airport, 14 April 2001. Kes Hillman Smith and Eric Edroma are finally on their way home, Smith to Nairobi in Kenya and Edroma to Kampala in Uganda. Four internal flights cancelled, eight meetings in Addis Ababa, Bahir Dar and Gondar, a six-hour drive on a dirt track and a donkey trek to visit the Simien, all in the space of five days. A job well done. Sent to Ethiopia by UNESCO and the IUCN, the two conservationists are now in a position to suggest four reforms to improve the management of the park. One: the 'extension' of its borders. Two: 'effective control' to ensure more 'efficient' regulation. Three: 'reduction' of the local population. Four: 'realignment' outside the park of the road which runs through it.[1]

Such measures were a common element of African conservation. They were identical to those imposed under colonial rule: transform more land into protected areas, reinforce already repressive laws, remove local people and prevent them from moving around freely. Only the vocabulary of authority had changed and yet nobody appeared shocked by these injunctions.

The prestige then associated with the world of consultancy was a key factor. Kes Hillman Smith was not merely a British woman who was more interested in African animals than in Africans. Having taken Kenyan citizenship, the zoologist was known throughout the world for her work in the national parks threatened by the war in central Africa. And Eric Edroma was more than just a Ugandan leader who would use nature to consolidate the income and power of an authoritarian state. Rewarded by UNESCO for his work as head of the Uganda Wildlife Authority, he taught conservation at Makerere, the country's most prestigious university.

The formulaic approach also explains the success of community-based conservation. 'Participative management', 'citizen consultation', 'shared analysis', 'respect for intercultural links', 'local partnership space': the international discourse is now cloaked in such technical respectability that it can no longer be challenged.

But words cannot hide the reality of the situation, and those who defend the community are also those who criminalize it. The reality is shocking but the archives do not lie: the international institutions are not protecting nature in Africa. They are simply protecting a colonial idea of Africa.

The spectre of degradation

United around the community-based ethic, the expert and the leader continued to work together. Between 1996 and 2017, UNESCO consultants carried out seven assessment missions in Ethiopia. They represented the IUCN, the Frankfurt Zoological Society, the WWF or the University of Bern, and their conclusions were always the same, notably that the park had deteriorated. In the meantime, in the annual meetings of its World Heritage Committee, UNESCO validated their analyses: tighter regulation was needed in order to halt the process.

The consultants then returned to Ethiopia to help the authorities draw up 'management plans'. They defined the measures to be put in place, which the federal authorities then implemented in the field. Thanks to an annual budget of 200,000 euros largely provided by the United Nations, the park guards were able to restrict the use of the site. They patrolled the Simien on a daily basis and prevented local people from extending their fields and their pastures. They also sanctioned anyone caught hunting, cutting wood or constructing new houses.

From the headquarters of UNESCO in Paris to the village of Gich in the Simien, all this work was based on a single sledge-hammer argument: the imminent disappearance of the Walia ibex, the wild mountain goat for which the Simien Park was widely known but which was also the reason why local people were being penalized.

In 1963, Leslie Brown counted 150 Walia within the park. The 'situation is serious', he told UNESCO, 'but far from hope-less'.[2] In 1978, John Stephenson counted 300. He was very much afraid that the species would be 'lost forever', as he wrote to the WWF. Thirteen years later, in 2001, Eric Edroma and Kes Hillman Smith recorded 450 Walia. This figure, they reported to UNESCO and to the IUCN, must 'reinforce the need to reduce or exclude human presence'.[3] In 2006 it was the turn of Guy Debonnet, Lota Melamari, and Bastian Bomhard to suggest that the ibex was under threat. For the 625 specimens in the Simien, they informed UNESCO, the presence of cattle in the park represents 'a catastrophic risk of disease transmis-sion'.[4] Finally, in 2017, without citing any other figures, Jeager Tilman announced to the IUCN that although ibex numbers appeared 'stable' since the resettlement of the village of Gich, the situation nevertheless remained very 'fragile'.[5]

The experts associated this fragility with the destruction of the Walia's natural habitat by a constantly growing human population: 1,500 people were living in the park in 1963, a little over 5,000 in 2016. Not one of the consultants picked up the error. According to their own calculations, in fifty years the number of inhabitants had multiplied fourfold, exactly as had the number of ibex. Moreover, as is evident from one of the only in-depth studies carried out on the subject, the population of ibex had been increasing at a steady rate from the first count in 1963. The numbers only dropped on two occasions, notably in 1973 and in 1985.

These dates correspond to the deadliest famines in contemporary Ethiopian history, two periods of crisis which drove local people to hunt an animal which was barely edible and difficult to kill. In fact, the more people's living conditions improved, the more Walia there were. But the experts failed to make the connection. They preferred to ignore their own figures and to maintain a position of principle: the local people would end up causing the ibex to disappear and would therefore need to be resettled.

The same declinist analysis governed the management of forests within the Simien. In 1978, Swiss geographer Peter Stähli compared photographs of the park dated 1954, 1964 and 1975. In his view, the local inhabitants had exhausted the soil to such an extent that they had been forced to abandon fields cultivated at altitudes of 3,200 metres and move higher up, to an altitude of 3,700 metres, in order to farm other land. For Stähli, this was the cause of the destruction of 85% of 'original forests'. And if this expansion of agriculture was not stopped, he was convinced that the catastrophe would be 'inevitable'.[6] The zoologists Bernhard Nievergelt, Tatjana Good and René Güttinger carried out the same study in 1998 – with, in addition, photos of Simien dated from 1983, 1994 and 1996. They, too, described the utterly 'devastating' effects of farming practices and, in turn, recommended measures to 'drastically reduce the extensive impact of man', in particular, according to them, in Gich.[7]

The argument was fallacious. What did those photographs actually show? The high ground which was wooded in 1954 was indeed bare in 1996. By contrast, however, the lower-lying land which had been bare in 1954 was wooded in 1996. And if the tree heather had indeed disappeared on the lower-lying lands which had been cleared for grazing, it had, on the contrary, reappeared on higher ground where agriculture had expanded. In fact, a system of rotation was in place in which the higher land was cleared when the lower-lying land was being reforested and the lower-lying land was cleared when reforesting took place further up.

Various historians have consulted the archives and investigated in the field in order to assess the truth of this kind of photographic study. In 1998, in the Wollo province, a few hundred kilometres south-west of the Simien, Donald Crummey observed that the clearing of lands as a result of pastoralism coincided with the planting of coffee trees in other fields, which then created shady zones where other plants could subsequently grow.[8] More widely, in 1999, James McCann pointed out that on the high plateaux of East Africa, the agro-pastoralists who practised intensive farming all used conservation methods of various sorts. Depending on the different contexts, these included the construction of micro-terraces, irrigation channels or the use of manure to fertilize garden plots.[9]

The same practices were also present in West Africa. Melissa Leach and James Fairhead even demonstrated that in the twentieth century, in Guinea, Ivory Coast and Togo, in areas where international experts claimed that 60 to 90% of 'primary' forests had disappeared, the forest cover had in reality increased. Like everywhere else, moreover, contrary to claims made by conservationists, people have adapted to their environment. If national and transnational companies did indeed ravage the forests and reduce the amount of habitat available to wild animals, in the majority of cases, agro-pastoralists were not guilty of destroying nature. In Ethiopia, as in Africa as a whole, given that their survival depended on it, they were generally anxious to conserve nature.[10]

A useful myth

The criminalization of African peasants (they were destroying forests everywhere) should not be replaced by their glorification (they were protecting the forest everywhere). That said, a study of the local history of these neo-Malthusian narratives reveals that not a single global study has ever genuinely analysed the ecological state of Africa, a continent three times bigger than Europe, and where people have sometimes reduced and sometimes extended their forests. Retracing this history is a way of gaining understanding. Why does the myth of the African Eden still endure? Because it serves both those who invented it and those who turn it into a reality.

This myth was so deeply rooted in western societies that, in 2007, Al Gore received the Nobel Peace Prize for his contribution to the fight against climate change, thanks to his book *Earth in the Balance* (1992) and his film *An Inconvenient Truth* (2006). His work is, however, riddled with absurdities. Gore describes, for example, the disappearance of forests in Ethiopia, stating that, in or around 1900, 40% of the country was forested but, forty years later, the figure had dropped to only 1%. The former American vice president claims that 'the effects of the prolonged drought [. . .] have combined with the incompetence of its government to produce an epic tragedy: famine, civil war, and economic turmoil'.[11]

Like the analyses provided by western conservationists in the African national parks, Gore's arguments did not stand up well to analysis. In the Ethiopian case, the figures cited turned out to be a complete fabrication. No study on the changes in forest cover had been conducted on a national scale, either using dendrochronology (annual growth rings in tree trunks) or using palynology (the density of pollen in the soil). As for climate change, if Gore did indeed identify its social effects with a rare precision, the American is considerably vaguer when it comes to describing the causes. Nothing is said, for example, about Apple or Google. These organizations have a gigantic ecological footprint, and yet Gore finances them and sits on their management committees. In other words, he is as much involved in the destruction of nature as in its conservation.

This encapsulates the incoherence of sustainable development. Having failed, in the northern hemisphere, to conserve the natural resources and landscapes which their life style has destroyed, many westerners are determined to be seen to be 'doing something' in the southern hemisphere.[12] This is why international policies have consistently failed to break with the past. In all Africa's protected zones, the colonial character of conservation is still 'the elephant in the room'.[13] For the West needs to believe that down there in Africa something still exists which can no longer be saved at home: a garden of Eden where there is still space for untamed nature and wildlife.

The African states also need this myth, though for different reasons. In each country in the continent, those in power are keen to profit from the revenues generated by tourism. Recognition from UNESCO, the IUCN and the WWF constitutes an additional source of attraction, and consequently any recommendations made by the international conservation institutions are applied to the letter – especially when those same organizations decree that their heritage is 'in danger'. Any such suggestion will be picked up by travel guides, from the *Guide du Routard* to *Lonely Planet*, and that is something African authorities cannot afford to happen. In order to attract visitors, Eden must remain unblemished.

Of course, in certain countries, tourist activity is structurally limited. This is the case in states which are considered too unstable, such as Sierra Leone or Eritrea, or those which are too poor, like Nigeria and Ethiopia. With 3,500 visitors per year, the Simien, for example, brings in less than 2 million birr per year to the Ethiopian government (i.e. 100,000 euros).[14] Conservation is nevertheless a useful means of improving the country's image in the eyes of the outside world. It brings with it a certain degree of respectability vis-à-vis the international institutions, and, as a knock-on effect, enables them to benefit from the technical and financial help these can provide. Thanks to food and military aid from the United Nations, Europe and the United States, many African states find themselves able to exercise firmer control over their populations. The sacrifice of the inhabitants of a national park is therefore a small price to pay in order to demonstrate to the world their willingness to follow the international criteria of 'good governance'. In this respect, too, Eden may well be an illusion but it is nevertheless very useful.

Parks for people, against the people

Let us return to Ethiopia. In reality, the government had little choice. If it wanted the Simien region to gain worldwide recognition, it needed to expel the inhabitants. In itself, eviction was not a problem for the authorities. Since the end of the nineteenth century, the modern Ethiopian state has displaced groups of people in order to build dams, exploit agricultural regions and impose its power on new territories.[15] The task of the new Ethiopian leaders consisted therefore in combining authoritarian practices – their own – with the norms of conservation as laid down by the international institutions.

In order to achieve this, in 1995, they decided to establish a National Strategy for Conservation. Over a period of two years, a dozen or so governmental agencies drafted a policy which was in line with the rules drawn up in Rio by the Convention on Biological Diversity. Their task was completed in 1997, and Ethiopia informed the conservationists that it was ready: the Federal Republic wished to implement a 'sustainable social and economic development [. . .] so as to meet the needs of the present generation without compromising the ability of future

generations to meet their own needs'.[16] The text was in line
with international norms.

As was its implementation. In accordance with the standards of the new conservation in Africa, the community-based
strategy led to the launch of 'integrated development projects'.
In the Simien National Park, this programme was financed by
the Austrian embassy and began in 1997. The park managers
embarked on the construction of three camps for their guards,
but work was cut short by the outbreak of war with neighbouring Eritrea in 1998. It would be a further two years before
the Ethiopian authorities could re-start the project under the
supervision of Marco Keiner, a consultant sent by Falch, a
company based in Landeck, Austria.[17]

The Ethiopian government promised jobs and financial
compensation to any local people willing to accept resettlement. But to no avail. They needed to try a different strategy.
The government then attempted to lure the local population
across the park boundaries, into a buffer zone where everybody would benefit from development aid.[18] Between 2003 and
2007, more than a million euros was invested in this zone.
With the help of the Austrian embassy, the Ethiopian managers provided local people with cattle, hives, saplings and seeds
suitable for horticulture. They employed villagers to construct
eucalyptus nurseries and reservoirs, and offered training to
anyone interested in the management of micro-businesses.[19]

Inside the park, on the other hand, local people did not
receive any aid. Quite the opposite, in fact. While they were
constructing wooden guesthouses and composting toilets for
tourists,[20] the guards put in a check-point at the western entry
to the park, followed by two new camps near the eastern exit.[21]
In a number of valleys, they imposed a now total ban on pastoralism.[22] Finally, they uprooted all the eucalyptus trees planted
by local people to provide firewood for cooking and heating.[23]

All these measures provoked the anger of the local population. 'They're trying to wear us down,' said Ali, in April 2007.

'They want us to get poorer and poorer so that we have no other alternative except to leave our villages and go and live somewhere else. I'm staying. I was born here in Gich and I want to die here.'[24] The project ended in failure at the close of 2007. The inhabitants of the park refused to leave. Like Ali, they rejected this global policy which resulted in them having to choose between a rock and a hard place, between abandoning their mountains in the name of integrated development, and remaining in their villages to be punished every day in the name of conservation.

People living in the area around the park were not necessarily any better provided for, either in Ethiopia or in Africa as a whole. At the beginning of the 2000s, in the Ugandan parks, for example, although local people profited handsomely from tourism revenues, they harboured feelings of strong resentment against environmental agencies which gave them money, but deprived them of the right to have any say in the management of their territory. Conservation policies remained exclusive.

At the same period, in Zimbabwe, local districts were now managing their parks themselves. Thanks to CAMPFIRE (Communal Areas Management Programme for Indigenous Resources), a WWF project, the natural environment was managed from within the village itself. But the district leaders were simply substitutes for central government since it was they who set out the laws, restricted agro-pastoral activities and collected revenues generated from tourism. The parks remained an exclusion zone.

Other scenarios were possible. In Namibia, for example, the people living in the parks stopped protecting wild animals because of the sacred value they attributed to them. Instead, each animal was given a monetary value in proportion to the attention it attracted from foreign visitors. Nature was therefore no longer conserved for its own sake. Instead, it relied for its protection on the continued presence of tourists.[25]

Put another way, community-based conservation never achieved its social mission. Perspectives had changed radically since the end of colonization. From the Maghreb to southern Africa, the notion of ecological balance had been replaced by that of ecosystem services: in other words, systems where all living beings, both humans and 'non-humans', cohabit in a dynamic way.[26] From Africa to Asia, the actors of conservation at that time attached too much value to anything relating to 'local people' and to the link between them and nature.[27] Except that community-based conservation always comes from above. The national parks are made for the people but there has never been any suggestion that the people should be involved in their conception.

The disintegration of the community

The problem is that the professionals who formulate such discourses are also the ones who end up imposing them, in their own way. Key figures in globalization, these are the driving force behind the new planetary Leviathan described by Edgar Morin in *La Méthode*: 'a mega-machine driven by an international elite of leaders, managers, experts, economists [. . .]. Confident that it holds the key to history, it is convinced that it is working for the good of all.'[28] And in the African national parks, even if these women and men never say it out loud, the perceived truth would be that the peasants are incapable of taking care of their environment.

In the Simien region, the attitude of the Swiss experts is instructive. When Nievergelt, Good and Güttinger arrived in the park in 1998, they recommended the resettlement of its inhabitants. Yet these conservationists were by no means devoid of emotion: 'It is sad to see the warm and friendly Simen inhabitants are causing serious damage to their surroundings,'[29] wrote the three zoologists.

Then, in 2005, it was the turn of Hans Hurni to assess the state of the park. The geographer made the same observation and the same recommendation as his colleagues. He was, however, somewhat more optimistic: '[T]he author is confident – in view of the motivated leaders he met along the route, as well as interviews he conducted with numerous peasants who are apparently taking their fate into their own hands – that both will further work together towards sustainable development.'[30]

According to these Swiss experts, the Ethiopians were little more than overgrown children on the point of finally putting into practice what the world had been teaching them for so many years. And, in a sense, they were not completely wrong. For since 2005, the park managers had carried out an intensive campaign to raise awareness of sustainable development.

Like good governance, this watchword lay at the heart of the new conservation ethic. Over the course of the previous twenty years, it had cropped up on a regular basis in all the reports produced by international experts and African leaders. From the World Bank to the tiniest NGO in the field, not a single institution failed to work along these lines. In the Simien, between 2005 and 2009, the guards organized more than 3,200 awareness-raising meetings. They went from village to village explaining to the inhabitants the importance of the national park and its laws: 'the park is your heritage', 'UNESCO is protecting the park', 'cutting down trees is forbidden', 'hunting is forbidden', 'the park will provide you with jobs', 'the park belongs to you', 'you should benefit from the park'.[31]

The guards constantly reiterated the same slogans and eventually, thanks to their newfound 'awareness', the local people ended up assimilating these values. As a result, social life in the Simien Mountains was quickly transformed. Over the course of the last fifteen years or so, many local people have abandoned agro-pastoralism in favour of jobs such as guides, cooks or muleteers (tourists have to pay for the mule which transports their equipment and for the muleteer who leads it on the walking trail).[32] Those who are refused jobs in the park can also pass themselves off as official guides for tourists. Despite the risk of a prison sentence, by proposing lower rates than the ones fixed by the park, they are sure to be in demand with visitors.[33]

Many children also neglect morning school and afternoon work in the fields. For them, and for their parents, who sometimes encourage them to do so, it is far more profitable to go out and beg for money from tourists.[34]

Finally, those agro-pastoralists who continue to cultivate their fields have taken to denouncing their neighbours. By providing the guards with the names of villagers who have hunted small game or cleared a section of forest, these people hope to obtain financial rewards and eventually, who knows, perhaps a job as a guard.[35]

This gradual decline of the community is the common lot of tourist enclaves throughout the continent. This phenomenon was first observed thirty years ago by the geographer Georges Cazes. He noted that since the former imperial territories had become the new holiday destinations for the West, domination had been replaced by a process of disintegration.[36] The place of Africans in nature is still one assigned to them by the outside world, but it is no longer one of subservience. Their role now consists in making a living by escorting tourists in quest of wild and beautiful spaces.

The people sacrificed to world heritage

Africa does not have a monopoly on this neoliberal transformation of nature. In many protected zones in the West, conservationists require those who live there to concentrate on protection rather than exploitation. Their lives should revolve around rural traditions rather than aspiring to be modern and urban.[37] Yet not a single country in the Global North has had to deal with the kind of norms enforced in Africa. The famous 'criteria' imposed on Ethiopia by experts are an indicator of the violence of this global conservation of Africa.

In 2006, the managers of the Simien Park extended its boundaries to the east and west. This meant there were more Walia in the core zone. At the same time, they narrowed the northern and southern boundaries and, as a result, fewer villages were included within the park.[38] This was a clever move since it met two of the conditions imposed by UNESCO for the removal of the Simien Park from the List of World Heritage in Danger. Criterion 1 called for the park to be extended, and its surface area had now grown from 210 to 410 square kilometres. Criterion 3 insisted that the number of inhabitants be reduced: the park's population was now no more than approximately 3,400.

As for the 1,400 inhabitants now 'outside' the park as a result of the shrinking of the northern and southern boundaries, these found themselves plunged into a truly Kafkaesque existence. Their villages were now in the buffer zone, on the other side of the park boundaries. Their fields, however, were still in the core zone. These agro-pastoralists therefore had the right to farm land where they did not possess any (in the buffer zone), and the duty to stop farming the land that was formerly theirs (in the core zone). An utterly absurd situation.[39]

Then came criterion 4, the realignment of the road. Constructed with the help of the British, in 1975 this road extended for a distance of 30 kilometres. It was destroyed as a result of the civil war in the mid-1980s, and in 1995, the new leaders of the Ethiopian Revolutionary Front decided to rebuild it and to extend it further eastwards. UNESCO and the IUCN objected to this plan in 1996, on the grounds that the park was still in danger and the road would only further aggravate the situation.[40]

But the prime minister refused to give way. Like many of the soldiers in the Front, Meles Zenawi had fought the Derg in the Simien area. Local people had provided his men with arms, shelter and food and the road would be their reward. Ethiopia decided therefore to continue the work on the road. Eleven years later, in 2007, the road extended across the park from west to east covering a distance of 75 kilometres. To the north it went as far as the town of Beyeda, and to the south, to Mekane Birhan.[41] Faithful to their electoral policy, which promised electricity to all rural regions, the leaders of the Front also decided to construct a power line alongside the road.

The situation became more complicated in 2008. At this point, UNESCO issued Ethiopia with an ultimatum. Without a genuine commitment by the authorities to 'realign' the road and the power line outside the park, the Simien would remain on the List of World Heritage in Danger.[42] This tension between experts and leaders is at the root of the bizarre situation in which the inhabitants of the Simien have found themselves living ever since. In January 2019, in the centre of the park, a power line could be seen running alongside a road which only Ethiopians were authorized to use. And outside the park, just a few kilometres away, workers could be seen constructing another road and another power line.[43]

These new infrastructures would replace those of the core zone, once all the inhabitants had been resettled. In the meantime, the introduction of stricter measures limited the use of the sites. This corresponded to criterion 2, imposed by the IUCN and UNESCO, which called for 'effective conservation'. This last criterion tipped the park into violence.

The violence was initially all too real. In Debark, Adi Arkay and Jenamora, the three districts with jurisdiction over the Simien, the courts imposed sanctions on local people found guilty of poaching. In 2007, for example, two villagers were punished with prison sentences: eight years for killing a fox, one year for killing a hyena.[44] Other inhabitants were found guilty of cutting down trees. In May 2008, three people were given fines of 1,800 birr each for this offence (75 euros at the

time, the equivalent of nine months' salary).[45] Agro-pastoralism
was also sanctioned. The authorities confiscated the harvest of
anyone who had extended their fields, and imposed fines on
shepherds from the buffer zone who had allowed their livestock to graze in the core zone.[46] Finally, on a regular basis,
the guards destroyed the wood and mud houses built by young
men hoping to start families.[47]

This criminalization of everyday life became part of a genuine 'war for biodiversity'. We owe the metaphor to James
Wolfensohn, Mohamed El-Ashry and Peter Seligmann: the
first was president of the World Bank, the second was chairman of the Global Environment Facility at the UN and the
third was founder and chairman of the American organization
Conservation International. The three men officially launched
this 'war' in 2001. In reality, however, the international institutions in question had been funding the militarization of African
national parks since the mid-1980s.[48]

Like Britain, the United States or the WWF, they were sup-
plying equipment and weapons to African states. The goal was
to combat organized networks of poachers operating within
the national parks – except that the agro-pastoralists ended
up being the real victims of this war. In Tanzania, during
September 1997, when the region was threatened by famine,
the guards of the Serengeti Park shot villagers who had come
to hunt small game. In Malawi, between 1998 and 2000, park
guards raped at least 250 women, and killed more than 300
people. During the same period, there were almost 400 deaths
in the protected zones of Zimbabwe, Kenya and Botswana, all
at the hands of park employees.[49]

In common with many other protected areas in Africa,
Ethiopia was spared brutality on that scale. Moreover, as in
the rest of Africa, the inhabitants of the Ethiopian national
parks were less and less inclined to oppose the institution.
The authorities did indeed register some acts of resistance
in the Simien Park, including the burning of a (re)afforested

plot,[50] a check-point being forced[51] and a villager striking the
guard who had just killed his dog,[52] but no further attempts to
wipe out Walia were reported. For the violence displayed by
the authorities was now real and symbolic. Not only were the
inhabitants constantly subjected to laws and restrictions, but
they had also begun to assimilate the values of the park. And
these values were of a rare brutality: agro-pastoralists had no
place in a world heritage site – that is to say, in a site considered to be amongst the most beautiful known to the human
race. The local people had listened to and learned these values
and had ended up assimilating them fully.

The case of the village of Arkwasiye is an indicator of
this change of attitude. Situated on a ridge in the east of the
park, between two mountain ranges, Arkwasiye constituted a
threat to 'a wildlife corridor', according to the terminology of
UNESCO and the IUCN. As a result, in 2006, Guy Debonnet,
Lota Melamari and Bastian Bomhard recommended the resettlement of the 167 households in the village.[53] And, for the first
time, the inhabitants accepted. In 2009, under the supervision of the Austrian development agency and the park guards,
they destroyed their houses with their own hands. Then, once
Arkwasiye had been demolished, the inhabitants left and
moved to a new village 2 kilometres further east, on the Kayit
plateau.[54]

It was a double victory. The Ethiopian authorities had resettled the second most populated village in the park, and it had all
been done on a voluntary basis – the inhabitants had realized
that there was no place for them in a world heritage site.[55] The
international institutions could therefore be satisfied. Experts
no longer needed to dictate matters since their views were
now widely accepted. Because they defined the global problem
(deterioration), it was legitimate for them to also determine
the policy to apply at a local level (expulsion).

In Africa, as in South-East Asia and Latin America, the discourse used by the experts is always the same: the protection

of all (humanity) sometimes necessitates the sacrifice of some (the local people).[56] This is the case in the African national parks, as leaders in quest of recognition have explained to their local citizens. 'The government has taught us well,' Samuel told us, a few months after his resettlement from Arkwasiye. 'This is a park. UNESCO has a duty to protect. We understood that we had to leave.'[57]

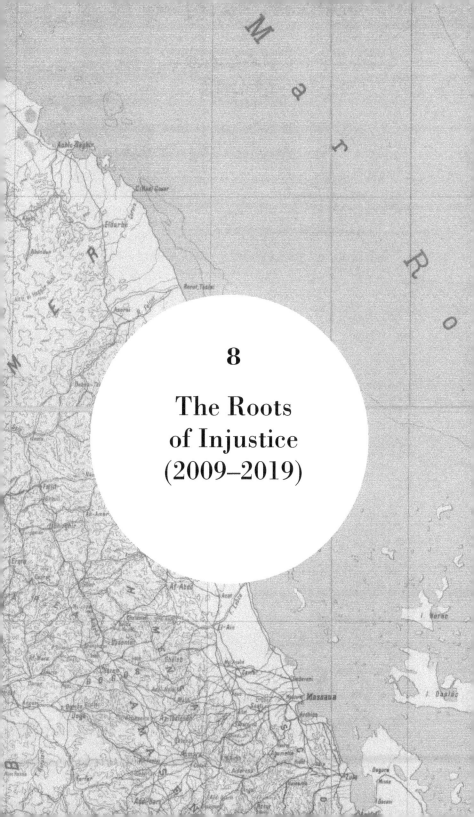

8

The Roots
of Injustice
(2009–2019)

Ambaras, Simien Mountains, 3 January 2019. Philippos is going to have to leave the natural landscape in which he lives. 'They' told him, and as in Samuel's case, the message is perfectly clear: the land belonging to his village is situated inside the park; no one must live there; his village will therefore be resettled. What Philippos fails to understand is the rationale behind this argument. For him, 'protecting nature means that everyone has enough to eat, that everyone can make a living from the resources passed on from father to son'. It is not surprising then that 'preserving the resources and then no longer having any resources, that is what troubles [him]'.[1]

The idea disturbs him all the more because he knows what awaits him once he leaves. 'The people from Gich who were resettled have nothing to eat. They don't have any bread,' Philippos says. He is not mistaken. The inhabitants of Gich abandoned their village in 2016 and since then, like those of Arkwasiye before them,[2] they have become poorer.[3]

This is the most difficult aspect of this book. Even today, the story it pieces together remains a shocking one. More and more historians are turning their attention to the global politics of nature in Africa. But, most of the time, the work we submit

for publication is subjected to furious criticism by those whose
job is to evaluate it. One anonymous reviewer of an article
I had written recently accused me of 'biased references' and
of a 'reductive and caricatural stance'. He advised me above
all to abandon the argument of an 'unjust' conservation. Yet
injustice does indeed exist and its story demands to be written,
its workings exposed. That is what will be investigated in this
final chapter.

Experts produce socially destructive policies because they
refuse to listen to those they claim to be helping. We need
therefore to take the opposite stance and genuinely, for once,
give a voice to those who interact with nature on a daily basis:
the women and men who live in it, look after it and visit it.
Where the archives relate a tale of violence, these anonymous
voices tell us how things really are. They alone can really make
clear to us why the colonial past weighs so heavily on the present reality of the African national parks.

A new poverty

Let us first be clear about the precise nature of the injustice we
are referring to. In 2009, experts from the IUCN once more
recommended the resettlement of all the inhabitants of the
Simien Park.[4] Then, in 2010, the UNESCO World Heritage
Committee again requested that Ethiopia follow these recommendations.[5] And finally, in 2014, the Ethiopian authorities
complied. They informed the Simien agro-pastoralists of an
imminent resettlement: the 3,480 inhabitants of the park
would have to leave, as would the 1,477 people living in the
buffer zone but whose land was located in the core zone of the
park.[6]

The resettlement of Gich was the first stage in this process.
In charge of the project were the United Nations Development
Programme and the African Wildlife Foundation. Intersocial

Consulting, an international consulting company, planned the various stages to be followed, and KfW, a German investment and development bank, provided the necessary funding. It was then the job of the park guards to ensure that the local people were willing to leave of their own accord. They obtained an agreement from them, in the form of a piece of paper signed with a cross, and in June 2016, the 2,508 inhabitants of Gich left their village. UNESCO had requested their eviction in 1963, and it had finally happened. All 418 families left the Simien Mountains behind them, bringing with them 5,000 head of cattle.

The Austrian Development Agency was the final actor involved in the project. At the very moment the inhabitants were leaving Gich, the employees of the Agency were completing work on two hiking trails for tourists in the park and fourteen outposts for guards. And when the villagers arrived in the town of Debark, 35 kilometres to the west, experts from the Agency provided training in masonry, carpentry and joinery, bee-keeping, embroidery, weaving and breadmaking. The aim was to allow the agro-pastoralists to make the transition to urban life.[7]

With nature on one side of the boundary and people on the other, this very sharp separation between conservation and development was a failure. The Ethiopian government was not particularly to blame. The resettlement had been prepared over a period of two years, and the inhabitants had received the compensation they were entitled to – a sum of money equivalent to the value of their houses, their cattle and their possessions – as well as a piece of land where they could settle and build a new house. The problem is that this kind of project is doomed to failure, whether in Ethiopia or elsewhere.

Michael Cernea, a sociologist at the World Bank, has prepared and monitored hundreds of resettlement programmes throughout the world. The result, he writes, is always the same: 'a vast number of displaced people have ended up worse off, poorer than they were before development projects displaced them'. In reality, no amount of compensation can replace what has been lost. Abandoning land improved over many years, losing access to common assets, the disappearance of mutual aid networks, low morale, loss of identity, food insecurity, increased morbidity, forced displacement – all of these, Cernea observes, are the 'equivalent of an earthquake that [. . .] plunges those affected on a downward poverty spiral'.[8]

The inhabitants of Gich have found themselves caught up in this cataclysm since the summer of 2016. And those who still live in the park and in the surrounding areas continue to be fined on a regular basis for cultivating land. Obliged to reduce the size of their fields and their herds, their income continues to decline. All the agro-pastoralists end up being forced to confront the social disruption inflicted by tourism.

This new poverty casts a shadow over the record of most African policies on nature. It is a well-recognized phenomenon in the conservation world. For more than ten years, in every country in sub-Saharan Africa where they operate, NGOs and international organizations have found themselves struggling to redress the secondary effects of community conservation.[9] That said, by focusing too closely on the symptoms, their experts forget to question the causes of the problem. Why does UNESCO pursue policies where the result is the exact opposite of its social objectives? Why, in Africa, does the global protection of nature constantly lead to injustice?

The everyday actors of conservation can provide an answer to these questions. Feven, Samson and Philippos live inside the park, Tesfa patrols it, Aron and Mike are two of the tourists who visit the park each day. We all met in the Simien Park in January 2019 and they set about disentangling for us the strands of the injustice which currently prevails in the politics of nature.

A different park for different people

The first element to emerge from our discussions,[10] a basic one but which nevertheless deserves mention, is that each of these different individuals has a different vision of the park.

Philippos sums up his vision: 'In the Simien we cultivate the land.' He lives in the village of Ambaras and his field is situated in the core zone of the Simien Park. He is satisfied with his life: 'We make a living thanks to lentils. We're happy here.' Samson and Feven share this vision of their local area. Agro-pastoralists, this couple, both aged 55, have spent their entire life in Gich. They have been in Debark for three years now and miss their village. 'Now the men work in cob and mud construction, and the women sew and sell baskets on the market. It doesn't suit us here,' says Feven. 'There's no milk, no butter, no sweet potatoes, just water like this [she indicates the container in which her daughter is boiling water].'

Their houses disappeared from the plateau of Gich in the summer of 2016 and since then the only people seen in the area are tourists. Westerners, like the majority of the 5,500 annual visitors to the Simien, Aron and Mike have spent two days in the park, as do most of the tourists. These two Canadians, both in their thirties, described the mountains as 'really amazing' and were undeterred by the presence of a guard at their side.

In accordance with the regulations, all tourists must be accompanied by one of the park guards. Tesfa is one of these. Born in the Simien, he has been a guard since 1980 and, according to him, the park is a now a conservation zone: 'In the past, the park had not been cleared of cattle and people. Now it is protected, free from all of that.'

Depending on their lives, their profession or their interests, each individual sees the Simien Park in his or her own way: an agricultural territory, a recreational space or an enclosed area protected from people, each has their 'own' protected zone. Nevertheless, in the public domain, one image takes precedence, and that is the one defined by UNESCO and legally endorsed by Ethiopia, which emphasizes that the park is a 'natural' space. Experts and leaders were unanimous on the need to preserve the natural state of the area in the early 1960s, and this vision, and the need to implement it, has not diminished with the passage of time.

Time passes; practices remain the same

The leading player in the field is the Ethiopian state, the *mengest*. In Amharic – the native tongue of the inhabitants of the Simien region and of at least 25 million Ethiopians – *mengest* means both the state and agents of the state. The Federal Republic may indeed have introduced a form of democracy, but for many Ethiopians, particularly those in rural regions, the *mengest* still remains sacred. Its authoritarianism is perceived as a reality, and a necessity. Its power is accepted because it is by its very nature above challenge. UNESCO, however, does not make allowance for this political context. It is not part of its role. Its objectives are universal and standardized, and perhaps, too, it prefers to believe the Ethiopian leaders when they state that the inhabitants of Gich left of their own accord. For the international experts who have to move around from one country to another, it is far more convenient to ignore the extent to which the concept of voluntary relocation can sometimes be devoid of meaning.[11]

The notion of community conservation is just as ambiguous. Tesfa, the park guard, does his utmost to implement this ethical code within the Simien Park. In response to each of our questions, he emphasized the need to raise awareness amongst the local people: 'Now, when you are involved in awareness raising, people know what you're talking about. They'll say to you: this park is our park, the lessons you have given us are true [. . .], and the mistakes made in the past are purely our own.'

Tesfa is unequivocal. His work is dictated by the catch-word of the new conservation: parks for people. But we are in Ethiopia and here 'the state is the people and the people are the state', as he puts it.

> It is because of the people that the park is called a park. Otherwise, it would be like clapping with only one hand [. . .]. If there were no people there would be no protection. [. . .] My work is about convincing people. [. . .] I give lessons and I get people involved. I teach people. They accept the lesson and say 'amen'. None of them shouts at you. None of them refuses to listen or tries to prove you wrong.

If the park does indeed belong to the local people, it is above all because the people belong to the state.

Philippos confirms this. He has cultivated land within the Simien Park for more than thirty years, and in his view, the authorities act as much for him as against him, and this is simply the natural order of things. 'Every day, we must shoulder our burdens,' he explains. Within the park, this expression[12] refers to all the various restrictions which permeate the daily lives of local people: confiscation of crops, bans on cutting wood, fines for extending their fields or for grazing their herds within the park. The burden is so oppressive that some people even look back with nostalgia to the time of the civil war. 'During the time of the *Derg*, bad things happened to us,' Philippos admits. 'The soldiers punished people, they shamed robbers, [. . .] it was the time of the red terror but the park was fine [. . .]. But today we have something new to carry. Now our burden means doing all this. Today we have our burdens. All of this has become the burden.'

The sense of constraint is omnipresent and systematic and yet this farmer does not reject the lessons instilled by the park guards. 'We just accept whatever they tell us. We are guards ourselves, we guard what is forbidden. [. . .] It's not just the guards who protect the park's riches, but we ourselves because we don't take them. Why? Because it's a forbidden zone.'

This testimony gives some measure of the influence exerted by the Ethiopian state. If the western experts learned the basics of the languages spoken in the countries their work takes them to – as they do when they go to the United States or to France – they would have a better understanding of what this community, which matters so much to them, really thinks. Philippos could help them understand that even though the park laws might represent a real burden, from the moment they come from the *mengest*, he simply has no choice but to accept and even defend them. Those who live in the rural areas of North Ethiopia have very little room for manoeuvre.

Like Philippos, for the inhabitants of Gich, now resettled in the suburbs of Debark, choice simply does not exist. Like his neighbours, Samson is now poorer than when he was farming his own land and taking his meagre herd of cattle to graze in the mountains: 'We are the ones who have been in the dark ever since we first arrived. Ever since we got here, we haven't been able to make a living.' We asked him why he thought the authorities had not allowed him to continue living in Gich. 'In their own interests,' he retorted. With a helpless air, Samson continued: 'It's so the park can get bigger. But we and the wild animals were living there on equal terms. We were living together and we were protecting them from fires and from poachers. It was thanks to us that foreigners could see them.'

Here, too, the lessons of awareness-raising have borne fruit. By dint of being educated by the guards, including Tesfa, with whom he grew up in the Simien region, Samson has internalized the values of the park. So much so that, even after being forced out, the former agro-pastoralist continues to pronounce the discourse he has heard so many times: even if he was cultivating the land, he was 'protecting' it, he assures us, for the park and for the enjoyment of 'foreigners'.

Samson's message here is that conservation may indeed have become community-based, but it has never stopped being authoritarian. Ethiopian power tactics have survived the passing years. If, at present, government agents see themselves as genuinely operating in the service of the community, they also continue to believe that the people should show them total obedience. And if the members of the said community now see themselves as the true guardians of the park, each inhabitant also continues to see it as an institution which has total power over him or her. Nature always operates from the top down.

And from outside, too. Visiting Ethiopia for the first time, Aron and Mike are two of the backpackers so often encountered in the country. 'Four years ago, we did a road trip in Africa with two other friends,' Aron tells us.

> We wanted to go from Cape Town to Cairo in a 4 × 4, but it ended up taking longer than we'd expected and costing a lot more, so Mike stopped in Malawi, and another friend stopped in Kenya, and [. . .] two of us went by bus from Nairobi to Dar es Salaam in Tanzania, and then to Dubai. We still wanted to visit the countries on the way to Egypt: Ethiopia, Sudan, South Sudan . . . and Ethiopia was the next country.

Their trip was therefore not just about Ethiopia, but about Africa.

Then they returned to the reasons why they had come to be interested in the Simien. 'It's certainly because of newspaper articles,' Mike said. 'Television, *Animal Planet*, programmes like that, [. . .] the *National Geographic* channel which shows the monkeys in the Simien Mountains . . . you see this and you think "Yeah! This is Ethiopia, right!?" And when you get there, you want to see it all with your own eyes.'

It seems, finally, that one more practice is also immune to the passage of time: the experience of travelling through the vast open spaces of Africa. The two Canadians displayed no signs of condescension or of paternalism towards the local people. It was simply that where the Simien peasants had their burden to bear, the two backpackers were burdened with more than a century of clichés. After Livingstone, Hemingway and Blixen, today the BBC, Disney and *National Geographic* encourage nature lovers to go to Ethiopia in quest of an 'Africa' which is wild and rich in fauna. Immersed in this western fantasy, the two visitors are unwitting defenders of the African Eden.

Beyond nature: absurdity

Aron and Mike were seeking something that has disappeared in their own country. They were in quest of 'nature'. As is the case in the majority of African languages, the word does not exist in any of the Ethiopian languages. In Amharic, the closest term to it is *täfätro*: 'what is created'. The whole concept of nature therefore can be traced back to the experts who first introduced it in Ethiopia. During the 1960s, the latter resorted tirelessly to the same vocabulary. The Simien is a natural asset, declared the conservationists. According to them, the park was constantly deteriorating as a result of deforestation, overgrazing and erosion. Even so, the landscape was still spectacular, the fauna exceptional and the flora extraordinarily rich.

Aron and Mike share a vision not dissimilar to that held by the experts. The two young men particularly appreciate 'the natural beauty of the area', as Aron explained: 'The landscape, the topography, all of that, the waterfalls – it was really amazing. I would just have liked to have seen a bit more wildlife.' Mike stressed that he did not know very much about the area before visiting it: 'You look at Wikipedia and it tells you what's in the park, and you say "Wow! Ethiopian wolves, leopards, lots of monkeys!"' Then there are the spectacular mountains themselves:

I think that for tourists it's the whole panorama that's easiest to identify as being something really unique. I read that in the Simien you can climb as high as 4,500 metres and I could just picture the landscape. And we heard that there were also lots of animals, so we said to ourselves, 'Both of those in one place!? We've just got to go there!'

In this natural environment, the visitors see the fauna and the landscapes but never any people. This perception stems in part from their own culture and, to a certain extent, from the work carried out by the park managers. So, for example, Tesfa makes a clear distinction between what belongs in nature and what should be kept outside the park boundaries: 'UNESCO says, "We want a park cleared of everything, of people, dogs, cattle . . . everything," and that's what we're doing, that's what needs to be done here.'

In order to understand more clearly what Tesfa thinks of this injunction, we asked him if, in his opinion, people could still continue to live in the park. His response was immediate: 'No. It's not possible to have both at the same time, it's different.' Then he explained in more detail:

What the law and the leaders say is that for it to be considered a park there mustn't be anything external to spoil it. [. . .] If not, people will see cattle, not wild animals. [. . .] UNESCO came here and they taught us that the park had boundaries. They said that nobody apart from the guards should go in, and that the guards' job was to protect the park within the boundaries, that people recognize the superiority of the law, and that from then on, anyone who went in would be caught.

According to Tesfa, nature is a world which needs to be kept free of people. He did, however, specifically attribute this definition to UNESCO. Our conversation then moved on to the role of international experts: 'I'm worth more than someone who has studied and who turns up with their diplomas, their master's,' the guard declared.

> I've got my own natural education. We went all over those mountains, we climbed up and down and then afterwards they asked us what results we had collected. The expert took all the information we had collected, and then, thanks to our efforts and our fatigue, he became even more important. Apart from that, we got nothing. For a salary of 1,000 birr per month [40 euros, the equivalent in purchasing power of 300 euros in France], a salary which wouldn't even buy us so much as a few sweets!

Tesfa nurses an open hostility towards the experts. This does not spring from a divergence of opinions since he shares their vision of wild natural spaces which must be emptied of their inhabitants. However, he resents the conservationists for taking the credit for his own hard work. The conservationists refuse to acknowledge his place in nature and it is this which Tesfa finds unacceptable. And that is where the problem lies.

On the face of it, what we are seeing here belongs in the realm of international cooperation and the unequal treatment of national and international employees. In reality, the conflict is a more complex one. For, over and above simple professional competition, it is above all a question of meaning. What does 'nature' mean? Or, rather, what significance is attributed to 'nature' when it is confined within a park, in the Simien or in any other African world heritage zone?

Samson had to leave the park because he represented a threat to the environment. But the former inhabitant of Gich considers that, on the contrary, he was looking after the area. 'It was when we were still there that the park looked its best,' he says.

> Today, it's dead. Now that the ground is no longer worked, there's nothing to retain the water, and there are no more cattle.

We made terraces, we built dams to hold back water, channels, we used fertilizer for crops, and we had a good life. [. . .] It's now that the park will be threatened. Because what animals need is people. They need smoke rising from the chimneys.

Put another way, Samson considers that he has a rightful place within nature. In his eyes, 'Nature is the white heather, the little monkeys, the Jinbar waterfall, it's the things which must not be touched, which have their own place, different from ours, and which live just like that. That's what nature is,' the former agro-pastoralist explains. He continues: 'And then, a few wolves, a few Walia ibex. They don't eat what belongs to us. They live alongside us; they don't touch us and we don't touch them. We live together in harmony. We don't lay a hand on any of the *mengest* stuff – the wild animals – but we work the land which gives us a living.'

Unlike Tesfa, Samson makes no distinction between nature and humans. Instead, in the world around him, he separates what is useful to people and what is not, with, on the one hand, the wild creatures, living freely, and, on the other, the land, which provides him with a living. Philippos, who still farms his plot of land within the park, near Ambaras, thinks along similar lines. In the course of a lively exchange, this farmer makes us see how nature does not mean the same thing for everyone:

'The authorities say that working the land, grazing animals, makes the soil bare and deteriorates it. What do you think of that?'

'To stop the soil disappearing, we make drainage channels for the water. [. . .] We don't let the water spoil the land. We build terraces.'

'But once you've made the channels, what do you do to stop the soil wearing away and being eroded?'

'If we've got channels to stop the soil disappearing, where else can the water go? The soil doesn't go anywhere when you've done what needs doing.'

'So do you think that the government, and UNESCO, are right to say that you need to leave the park in order to protect it?'

'Telling people to leave is not good. It's a burden.'

'But if the park didn't exist, would people hunt the monkeys and the Walia?'

'Why would they kill them? What would be the point in killing them? The monkeys don't come into the fields. The Walia live on the cliffs. Who goes on to the cliffs?'

'But if it was to find food? If the park wasn't supervised, wouldn't people hunt the Walia?'

'Aren't the Walia on the cliffs? How could people go there to kill them?'

'Couldn't you shoot them?'

'And how would you bring them back? Even if you killed one, how would you ever find it? There's no way of getting there.'

'And when people talk about "nature", what does that mean for you?'

'Nature is a resource. It's a resource. It's our livelihood. But it's also what is forcing us to leave our resources, in the name of those same resources. We have to fight for our resources. But now we're upset because we're being told we have to leave our resources for the sake of the resources. Because nature is a resource.'

This first-hand account explains why the number of inhabitants and the number of Walia are both on the rise. Local people do not hunt ibex except in times of famine. But what Philippos is describing is, above all, the aberration of this 'nature' which is being imposed on him. Why would anyone want to save land if it meant leaving it to be abandoned? For him, the answer to that question is simply absurd: it is preposterous, against all reason. Like all the inhabitants of an African park, Philippos relies on working the land for his subsistence. For him, therefore, nature is simply the backdrop for everyday life, not just a place to be visited temporarily; it is a territory that provides food and must be tended rather than an enclosed space that can simply be abandoned. Saving the resource in order to be deprived of resources cannot make sense.

A never-ending injustice

This absurdity leads directly to injustice. Before their departure, the people forced out of Gich were already amongst the poorest in Ethiopia. Today, they have become even poorer: 'I'm just dying here. We can't go on like this. It's either death or a return to our land,' exclaims Samson bitterly. 'If we do something, it will be to go back to our land and die there,' he announces, in front of his wife. Feven agrees: 'If we had stayed as we were before, with the wild animals up on the cliff and people at the bottom of the cliff, if we lived like that, things would be better. We think they should get rid of the park.'

But the decision does not lie in their hands. Moreover, it was only the authoritarianism of those in power that drove the inhabitants to leave voluntarily. 'We signed the papers,' Samson admits, before adding, with his head lowered: 'They beat us with sticks. They drove us out with sticks and metal bars. We couldn't even take our personal belongings.' Three years later, the memory of the resettlement is still painful. And today, in Ambaras, ten kilometres south of the now non-existent village of Gich, it is the turn of Philippos to fear expulsion: 'They said to them "take the money" and "leave". They signed and they left. I'm sure none of them will survive.'

This is why this farmer refuses to leave his village: 'We're not going. [. . .] They can kill us if they want, we're not going. Rather than go down there and have nothing, we prefer to stay where we belong. What could be better than that? What's better? To be as rich as you want down there, or to die in your own village?' The promises of financial compensation and professional training are not enough to convince him. He refuses to go and live in the town. 'It's not so bad here. There aren't any scorpions, or snakes,' he says, gesturing with his hands for us to look around at the surrounding countryside. 'The wind you breathe when you live here is good. We want to use the land they gave us here rather than go and live on land that belongs to other people. That wouldn't suit us. What suits us is our own land.'

Samson and Philippos both love their mountains. One misses them, the other clings to them as best he can. They also share the belief that the Ethiopian government is solely responsible for their eviction, past or future. Between the status of a national park and the classification as a world heritage site, the two men say that all they know is that 'UNESCO recognizes the Simien'.

Tesfa has a different view of the situation. 'I know that the park must be free of people,' the guide declares. He participated in the resettlement of the inhabitants of both Arkwaziye and Gich, and he knows why: 'To make more space for the wild animals. That's what they said when they did it. When UNESCO came to do its research, the park had not been cleared [. . .], Gich needed to be got rid of. Besides, the people of Gich have been a target for a long time now, ever since the time of Haile Selassie.'

If Tesfa seems to make a connection between the park, the government and the international institutions, the link remains a tenuous one. We asked him what he thought about the park being included on the UNESCO world heritage list, and his answer was tinged with uncertainty: 'Yes, UNESCO, yes . . . UNESCO says, "We want a park which is completely free of everything," but I don't know what UNESCO brings to the local people. If someone's going to leave a place, you have to offer them a lot of things, otherwise they will stay. [. . .] If they don't give them those things, I don't think that's good.'

He repeats this expression: the park must be 'free', and since it is still inhabited, it must be 'freed'. The decision comes from above, from UNESCO and the *mengest*, and Tesfa does not question the idea as such. On the other hand, he deplores the way things are done: 'If we said we work together in mutual trust then we should work in mutual trust!' he said, his voice getting angrier.

As for the two Canadian visitors, they knew nothing at all about the resettlement. We discussed it briefly and Aron was the first to react:

> I think . . . I'm not sure . . . I think that for the resources of the park, and to keep certain species alive, it's worth it. Of course I also think that it's painful being kicked out of your own place. [. . .] I think it's unfair for them, especially since they must already be disadvantaged. It's not fair for them . . . but men have fucked up the planet so badly that we have to do this kind of thing. It's really a shame that the ones who didn't fuck up the planet are the ones to be punished. These people do not cause much pollution, they just live from the earth [. . .]. It's like: 'Got to do it, but it sucks to do this to these people.'

In this disillusioned tone, Aron turned to his companion to ask his opinion. 'As far as I'm concerned, I can see myself protesting for them, saying "you can't do this"; but I can also imagine myself saying "we must do this",' Mike replied. Aron nodded his head in agreement before adding: 'Actually we can't win. It's a lose-lose.' Then he corrected himself: 'Or more a win-lose.'

With these words, Aron sums up the whole problem of nature conservation on a global scale. To our knowledge, geographers, political analysts and historians have reported incidences of enforced naturalization in the following countries: Guinea, Ivory Coast, Ghana, Togo, the Central African Republic, Gabon, the Democratic Republic of the Congo,

Eritrea, Kenya, Uganda, Rwanda, Botswana, Tanzania, Mozambique, Namibia and South Africa. And this grounded story of the Simien Mountains shows us in practical terms how, even today, the management of the African natural parks involves two opposing sides: the local people who want to live in a natural site and the conservationists who are determined to protect it. The former attempt to cultivate the land and the latter to prevent them from doing so by imposing sanctions, fines and prison sentences.

In the Simien, as in so many of the African parks, this reality represents injustice in the true sense of the term: being deprived of a right from which Others benefit, in the name of an ethical code defined by Others.[13] Driven out of their homes, or at least criminalized, those living in the parks are victims of a form of political discrimination, while the Others, those on the outside, still have the right to work the land. Penalized in the name of an ethic which is not their own, the inhabitants are also victims of a moral domination in that the Others, on the outside, have decreed that their natural spaces must be untouched, and that the attitude of the local people was so destructive that it justified their expulsion.

Steeped in neo-Malthusian prejudices, the western experts are the main drivers behind this injustice. Let us take one final look at the case of the Walia ibex. For the last fifty years, their existence has been the raison d'être of the national park, and their potential extinction the source of the violence suffered by its inhabitants. Numbering 150 in 1963, there are now 950 ibex in the Simien Park.[14] The Ethiopian managers recorded these figures in early 2017, the IUCN confirmed them a few months later and the UNESCO World Heritage Committee subsequently announced 'a considerable increase in the Walia population'.[15] However, in 2018, when this same committee drew up the list of the dangers threatening the Simien, it noted 'declining populations of Walia ibex'.[16] The myth of an African

Eden is so powerful that, even today, experts set more store by their beliefs than by their own figures.

The Ethiopian state makes use of this declinist mantra but is also a victim of it. For example, in 2008, the Ethiopian Wildlife Conservation Authority replaced the EWCO. Symbolically, the A replaced the O for Organization, and as a direct consequence the federal state removed the management of the Simien Park from the regional state of Amhara. The park would, from that point on, be managed by the federal authorities. These authorities had no choice, as they explained to the regional administrators: UNESCO requires world heritage sites to be managed by the highest authorities in the country.[17]

These two approaches to managing nature – international and national – are of course based on the same ideas, handed down from the colonial era: Africa is a wild, untouched land, just as it once was, but it is also overpopulated and damaged. This Africa makes no sense. Nature cannot both *be* and *have been* at the same time. It is impossible for African parks to be at the same time intact and yet destroyed, and for that to have been the case for almost two centuries. This image exists solely in the minds of experts, in the cinema, on television, in novels and nature magazines. Eden has never existed and therefore it can never be saved. UNESCO, the IUCN and the WWF may indeed do their utmost to invent it, but it will always be at the cost of injustice.

Conclusion

Sankaber, Simien, 6 January 2019. The tourists have spent their first night in the park. It is barely seven in the morning and the campsite is a hive of activity. Amongst the hundred or so tourists, from America, Europe and Australia, some are finishing breakfast, others are sorting out their tents, looking for sunglasses, sharing sun cream, stretching. Today's trek is Sankaber to Gich: a 17-kilometre hike, at an altitude of 3,800 metres and in scorching sun.

The hikers get themselves ready whilst, at the entrance to the camp, their guides are busy negotiating with the muleteers. All originating from the Simien, the guides went to live in the city to work in the tourist industry while the others remained in their mountains to farm the land handed down through generations. They all know each other, and yet each morning the same arguments begin all over again: will it be one mule or two?

The principle is a simple one. Each morning, ever since the park introduced its community policy in 2003, the government association Simien Eco-Trekking assembles any local people ready to hire out their mules to tourists. During the trek, the mules will transport the visitors' bags and the equipment supplied by their guide (gas canisters, pots and pans, plates, cutlery and food). The tariffs are fixed: 70 birr per mule and 100 birr per muleteer (in other words a combined cost of about 6 euros at current rates), and these earnings will be shared equally between the muleteers and the park managers. Except that, if the total weight of the pack is more than 30 kilos, the tourists have to hire a second mule, plus the services of a second muleteer.

The scales are not digital, but rely on an old-fashioned needle, and this morning, in Sankaber, the discussion centres on the equipment of a group of three Australian tourists. Their guide knows perfectly well that if his clients have to pay for two mules instead of one, they will deduct this surcharge from the tip they had planned to give him at the end of the trek. As a result, for him, there can be doubt whatsoever: the scales indicate less than 30 kilos. The muleteer does not agree. If the tourists have to hire two animals, he knows he will be able to bring his son along with him to drive the second mule, and they will be able to buy more food that week. For him, therefore, it is perfectly clear that the weight is well above 30 kilos.

The negotiations continue down to the last kilo. The two men begin to exchange insults before coming to blows. The muleteer slaps the guide, who then punches him in the face, and it requires Tesfa's intervention to separate them. The park guard weighs everything again. It will indeed be two mules and two muleteers. The guide does not dare to contradict him.

At the same moment, a few metres further away, another scene is being played out. Two tourists are finishing their coffees. The couple, both Americans in their forties, are accompanied by a Simien guide who is about 20 years old. One of the Americans has asked him how to say 'thank you' in Amharic, and the young man is teaching him the word – *amesegenalo* – saying it slowly for him. The American finds the word challenging and makes several attempts to pronounce it, causing the two men to laugh heartily. Then the guide abandons his client for a moment and goes off to hire a mule for their luggage and equipment. Still smiling about the incident, the American turns to his companion: 'Well, now it's my turn to teach him something,' he says, in a serious tone. 'They really need to learn about recycling. Have you seen all these plastic bottles!? They'll never make it. . . .'

The scene is a strange one. There is no drinking water for westerners in Sankaber, and, indeed, dozens of empty bottles are piled up on the ground at the entrance to the camp. Children from the neighbouring village will collect them at the end of the day. Tomorrow they will go into town to sell them to shopkeepers, who will use them to store and then sell petrol or methylated spirits. The environmental cost of the operation is a very real one. But compared with the ecological footprint of the tourists, it is trivial.

Before their trip to the Simien, the hikers have kitted themselves out. A tent with an aluminium frame to keep the backpack as light as possible; walking shoes and a waterproof and breathable Gore-Tex jacket; plus a fleece base layer for the chilly evenings in the high mountains: all of these involving manufacturing processes requiring the extraction and chemical processing of bauxite and petroleum and Teflon. As for the plane journeys of the 5,500 annual visitors to the park, given that a flight from Paris to Addis Ababa produces emissions of at least 0.5 tons of CO_2, their carbon footprint is equivalent to the annual destruction across the world of the ecosystems which are protected in the Simien Park.

The same contradiction applies in countless other national parks. In the United States, for example, in Yellowstone or Yosemite, tourists very often use highly polluting off-road vehicles to visit the parks. As in the Simien, many other countries in the southern hemisphere find themselves confronted with problems of violence provoked by the presence of foreign tourists. When the 'poor' allow the 'rich' to explore their world, they all expect to derive some kind of benefit from the encounter. The criminalization of those living in the parks is, however, largely confined to Africa. And it constantly harks back to the notion that Africa should be saved from the Africans. Without someone to teach them how to look after nature, as the American tourist remarked to his companion, 'they'll never make it'.

His concern may be perfectly sincere but it nevertheless raises some important questions. Between the 'they' of those who find themselves accused in this way and the 'I' of the person who has to help them, a whole world is emerging. What kind of world is it? In Africa's national parks, which world is protected, by whom, and for whom?

Which world is protected? An Eden, as in the colonial era. The UNESCO world heritage list is perhaps the most striking example of this naturalized vision of the continent. In 2019, the list featured 839 'cultural sites' and 213 'natural sites'. And the division is clear-cut. Ancient Europe numbers 414 cultural sites, that is to say, half of the world's cultural heritage sites; Africa has barely fifty-four. It is, however, home to a quarter of the natural heritage sites in the entire planet.[1]

For some, it is a matter of the genius of culture; for others, the beauty of nature. Director of parks in the Belgian Congo during colonization, then of parks in Zaïre under Mobutu, Belgian Jacques Verschuren observed this phenomenon in 1963: 'Europe has its cathedrals, preserved through the ages, Africa is proud to show its prodigious natural spectacles.'[2] Later, in 2001, in his role as consultant for UNESCO and the IUCN, Verschuren reiterated his remarks: 'Thanks to the Congolese, Rwandese and Burundians who protected their cathedrals – in the form of nature.'[3]

UNESCO is aware that it has for too long perpetuated this image of Africa. Anxious to remedy matters, in 2003, it created the concept of 'Intangible Cultural Heritage'. This category allows for the inclusion of societies which, unlike the Europeans, do not divide the world only into 'cultural' and 'natural' categories.[4] The problem is that the African parks which have been on the list of natural world heritage sites for forty years are still there today. And those inhabitants who have escaped eviction still continue to be penalized on a daily basis for their agro-pastoral activities. These parks are seen as the last traces of the African Eden, and it is still on this basis that they are protected.

By whom? By international experts, just as in the colonial era. The domination of colonial scientists was not strictly vertical and that of experts even less so. In several of the continent's parks, guards were killed by poachers, and, everywhere, African leaders made use of conservationists to keep better control over their populations. Yet the authority exerted by experts is by no means diminished. It is they who organize the management of the African parks and oversee their militarization, and, in certain countries, their power even extends to the formal administration of nature.

The Gabon is a textbook case of this. In 2002, President Omar Bongo set aside 11% of the country as national parkland (an area the size of Brittany, from Brest to Rennes). At the time he was assisted by American ecologist Michael Fay and British biologist Lee White, both these men having set off on a 'mission [. . .] to save Africa's Eden', as the *National Geographic* explained to its readers.[5] At that time, White was working for the Gabonese branch of the American organization the Wildlife Conservation Society.

Then, in 2009, Ali Bongo, who had succeeded his father as president, made White director of the National Agency for National Parks in Gabon. White quickly set up a 'National Parks Gendarmerie', an armed militia specializing in combating poaching. Finally, in June 2019, he became Gabon's minister of Forests, Sea and the Environment. Bongo and his followers gained respectability in the eyes of the international community, and White was able to pursue his mission. Fortunately, this 'real-life "Tarzan"' was there, to cite *National Geographic* once more, 'with the strength and resolve to conserve what's left of what is arguably Africa's most pristine Eden'.[6]

Protect, for whom? As in the colonial era, for those seeking to save in Africa the nature they are destroying elsewhere. On the one hand, there are the multinational companies. In Ethiopia, for example, it was a German development bank, KfW, which commissioned Intersocial Consulting to organize the resettlement of those living in the Simien Park. And throughout the entire world, mining and petrol companies like Rio Tinto, Total or ExxonMobil call on the services of this same Intersocial Consulting. The consultancy firm plans other 'sustainable development' projects for them. These companies exploit African resources on a massive scale, and, consequently, they do what they can to protect them within the national parks.

Then, on the other hand, but still coming from the West, there are the millions of individuals who set off to visit the protected zones of Africa, or who simply make occasional contributions to organizations such as the WWF. Their philosophy is generally the opposite of that of the multinational companies. But by defending the existence of these natural enclaves, in the form of the African parks, they, too, are seeking to exonerate themselves from the damage their lifestyles cause everywhere else. Believing that nature is protected where there are no people (in the parks) is also a way of condoning damage where people live (in the rest of the world). As long as authentic nature is protected down there, in Africa, we can continue to cause damage elsewhere to a world which is in any case already denatured.

Except that today there are no longer any perfectly untouched and totally intact spaces. History tells us that, in the case of Africa, this idea is a myth. First of all, in the nineteenth century, came the invention of the African Eden, a continent teaming with wild animals, flora and spectacular views. This illusion was quickly reinforced by misguided ideas, emerging at the beginning of the twentieth century, which suggested that this lush continent was under threat from deforestation, erosion and desertification. From the 1930s onwards, the national parks made this European dream a reality: in the form of conservation zones to be emptied of their inhabitants. And since then, international nature policies have played their part.

In 1960, when the IUCN, UNESCO and the FAO put together their African Special Project, they set themselves a goal, namely that the end of colonization would not signal the end of the natural parks established in the continent. The approach is no longer the same, of course. None of these institutions would dream of writing today, as did the IUCN, once their project was underway, that ecologists and consultants 'will work in Africa [. . .] to help Governments to help themselves'.[7] Yet the idea persists. Scientists and colonial administrators wanted the parks in order to protect an Eden-like Africa from destructive Africans, and, for the last sixty years, international experts have continued their work.

This state of affairs is all the more shocking in that, in Europe, these experts maintain an ethical stance which is quite the opposite of the one they impose on Africa. In France, for example, along the footpaths of the Cévennes National Park, signs explain to visitors why the park is included on the UNESCO world heritage list. Hikers passing through Le Pont-de-Montvert will find a display board on the Col de Sapet, where they can first of all read about the 'unique relationship between man and nature' in this area. The sign then goes on to explain that the Cévennes landscape is 'the heritage of 5,000 years of agro-pastoralism'. Finally, they will learn that within this park 'agro-pastoralism is particularly encouraged because it is indispensable to the survival of open environments threatened by the spread of forests, and therefore an essential element in maintaining biodiversity and the quality of the local landscapes'.[8]

The Ethiopians from the Simien region could scarcely imagine a better ethical approach. Sadly, their own park remains firmly under the banner of green colonialism. Experts from UNESCO, the IUCN and the WWF support agro-pastoralism in the Cévennes. In the Simien, however, they continue to stigmatize the agro-pastoralists. They defend the value of the open and cleared landscapes of the French countryside, yet in Ethiopia they stubbornly cling to the myth of the lost forest. Experts try to attenuate the socially damaging effects of the policies they impose in the African parks but their determination to naturalize Africa at any cost remains undiminished.

The same is true when it comes to the global conservation of nature across the whole continent. As long as the international institutions and their experts refuse to abandon this ecological policy which is the direct heritage of colonization, those living in the African national parks will continue to be victims of violence on a daily basis. And for them 'there's no time to lose', as Samson says. Like so many agro-pastoralists born in an African national park, Samson has spent his whole life being criminalized. And today, now that he has been resettled in a little town far from his mountains, he repeats the message with as much sorrow as anger in his voice: 'For us, it has become infernal. The situation can't go on. It's just infernal.'

Afterword
Looking Ahead

This book provoked two types of criticism in the French media. On the one hand, there were the regrets: it is a pity no solutions were proposed to mitigate the current inefficiency of conservation in Africa. And on the other hand, there were the accusations: with an author who seeks to discredit international cooperation, this work can only damage the ecological cause. It seems to me important today to say a few words in response to these attacks. My intention is not to address those responsible for them but rather to try to reflect objectively on their content in order to frame some potential solutions.

As early as September 2020, ten days after the publication of the book, the IUCN denounced what it referred to as 'false and unfounded allegations'.[1] A few weeks later, the number two at UNESCO also took exception to 'fake news' which would only 'mislead the public about the past and undermine the foundations of any possible action in the present'.[2] Following in the footsteps of the IUCN, UNESCO was resorting to an *as if* approach: as if it were not its own archives that had enabled me to conduct much of my research. And since then, faced with this story, their story, many experts have continued to express

their indignation: 'Africa is sovereign', 'poachers are slaughter-
ing big game in Africa', 'all over the continent, conservation
involves communities'. Of course.

Yes, African leaders are sovereign. That is indeed why they
know how to use the injunctions issued by the experts for
their own purposes. Thanks to the parks and the international
recognition which goes with them, they intend to revitalize
their tourist industry and plant the national flag in territories
which the state struggles to control, for example where there
are nomads, in areas of resistance or in the borderlands.

Yes, organized networks of poachers do indeed exist. They
have access to military technology, GPS trackers, all-terrain
vehicles and national and international political contacts.
Placing the blame on subsistence farmers and shepherds therefore amounts to turning a convenient blind eye. These farming
people have neither the human nor the technical means to be
part of such lucrative networks.

Yes, local communities are involved in conservation. But
how? In Uganda, those who benefit from tourism revenues have
no say in the management of their land and consequently are
today rejecting conservationist policies. In Ethiopia, following
the example of their elders, adolescents have given up school
in order to become tourist guides. These are now so numerous that many of them find themselves unemployed, without
any education or any possibility of retraining. In Namibia,
communities which were protecting wild animals because of
their sacred value now attribute a financial value to them, with
the result that when a worldwide pandemic deprives them of
tourists, interest in big game dwindles. In short, conservation
may indeed be 'community'-based, but it rarely ever attains the
social and ecological goals it claims to pursue.

This, I think, is the first lesson that we can take from reality:
whether we regret it or welcome it, the fact is that the global
policies for African nature are not working. For behind this
great 'Africa' of the expert's discourses, there are societies: that

is to say, different ways of thinking and of acting, actors with divergent interests, power games. In short: a complex situation. We need to recognize, therefore, that the global conservation model is by its very nature doomed to failure: because socio-ecological problems are always grounded, only grounded, and therefore differentiated, solutions can provide an answer to the current crisis.

History, and not the present, offers us another lesson. Why do experts from UNESCO, the IUCN or the WWF fail to support in Africa the farmers and shepherds whom they protect in Europe? Because they are convinced that, in Africa, the small-scale farmers are inexorably degrading the soil. It matters little that this idea has been handed down from a none-too-glorious past; the problem is that it continues to take its toll: the international institutions have a moral duty to admit their mistake. As long as they refuse to acknowledge the still existing burden of colonial perceptions of Africa and of Africans, no genuine solution can emerge. And yet, solutions do exist.

It is, first of all, imperative to abandon these beliefs and to turn at last to science. Rather than imagining that, all over the continent, Africa has lost its forest, its fauna and its flora, localized studies should be undertaken. These could take as their focus, for example, the long-term evolution of the forest cover in the tropical Congo, or in the high plateaux of Ethiopia, elephant numbers in Botswana or South Africa, or changes occurring in the desert lands of the Sahel. By conducting genuine scientific studies, country by country, natural environment by natural environment, as they have done in Europe, for example, not only can conservation experts gain understanding of the environments where they should or should not intervene, but they can also identify the causes of any changes.

This approach could then lead to a rational consideration of local communities. Rather than believing that, as a result of having insufficient land, farmers and shepherds end up exhausting it, conservationists should once again base their work on science and on a local scale. That would enable them, for example, to have a better understanding of arid environments and savanna lands, where non-equilibrium is the rule: the ecologies typical of sub-Saharan Africa are by nature unstable because they are susceptible to levels of water and nutrients in the soil, but also to how intensively that same soil is burned and grazed. This means that transformations of the environment are dependent on processes which are just as much internal (ecological) as external (social). It also means that, very often, slash-and-burn farming and grazing are just as likely to maintain environments as they are to damage them. And that implies that the farmers and shepherds are constantly adapting: to rainfall, the seasons and climatic variations. Understanding and recognizing the dynamic and social nature of African ecologies could therefore encourage conservationists not to exclude agro-pastoralists but instead to look at ways of improving their capacity to adapt. This could take the form of suggesting, for example, which seeds would be best suited to a particular type of soil, which transhumance route would be appropriate in a specific area, or what might be the ideal balance between agriculture and pastoralism at a particular moment of the year. By accepting the socio-ecological dimension of African environments, conservation experts could finally turn their words into actions and save the ecology by helping those best placed to save it.

This new approach would at last force the international institutions, environmental activists and each one of us to ask a single question: if those who make their living from subsistence farming are not in fact the ones responsible for the massive deterioration of the planet, whom should we be targeting? The question is a simple one and the response even simpler: the blame lies with consumerism and the capitalism that encourages it. Whatever our conception of time (whether or not we think about a world fit to pass on to future generations) and of society (whether or not we want to see an equitable distribution of resources), there is one fact that nobody can deny, namely that it is the capitalist exploitation of resources that is destroying the planet. Those in a position to decide global policies for nature in Africa should therefore, first of all, calmly accept the mistakes of the past, and then turn their attention to deciding which environments they should focus on and which populations they should work with. Having done so, they could at last find the courage to state the facts: only a radical reform of the world capitalist system can offer a solution to the current ecological crisis.

Recognizing that green colonialism still casts a shadow over the present is not difficult. Our vision of Africa and of Africans is a distorted one, and laying the blame on small-scale farmers is quite simply wrong. But if some refuse to hear this truth, it is because they seek to conceal another truth which is (truly) disturbing: if we want to fight for ecology, we have to shoulder our responsibilities ourselves. As Europeans, Americans, Africans, Asians, we can all decide to communicate with simple telephones instead of with smartphones, we can choose only to consume meat or fish a few times per month, we can accept being only allowed to travel by plane once a year, we can campaign for the car to be replaced by public transport. Everyone has a part to play. Or we can continue to blame the farmers and shepherds who live in a subsistence economy. The choice is ours.

Notes

Preface to the English Edition:
History as a Starting Point

1. T. Steinberg, 'Down to Earth: Nature, Agency and Power in History', *American Historical Review*, 107-3, 2002, p. 803.
2. S. Castonguay, 'Les rapports sociaux à la nature: l'histoire environnementale de l'Amérique française', *Revue d'histoire de l'Amérique française*, 60-1/2, 2006, p. 7.
3. J. MacKenzie (ed.), *Imperialism and the Natural World*, Manchester: Manchester University Press, 1990.
4. B. Gissibl, *The Nature of German Imperialism: Conservation and the Politics of Wildlife in Colonial East Africa*, New York and Oxford: Berghahn, 2016.
5. N.L. Peluso and M. Watts (eds), *Violent Environments*, New York: Cornell University Press, 2001.
6. C.C. Gibson, *Politicians and Poachers: The Political Economy of Wildlife Policy in Africa*, Cambridge: Cambridge University Press, 1999.
7. D. Hulme and M. Murphree (eds), *African Wildlife and Livelihoods: The Promise and Performance of Community Conservation*, Oxford: James Currey, 2001.

8. W. Cronon, 'The Trouble with Wilderness: Or Getting Back to the Wrong Nature', *Environmental History*, 1-1, 1966, p. 7.

9. W. Cronon, 'The Trouble with Wilderness: A Response', *Environmental History*, 1-1, 1996, p. 49.

10. W. Beinart, K. Middleton and S. Pooley (eds), *Wild Things: Nature and the Social Imagination*, Cambridge: The White Horse Press, 2013.

11. R. Grove, *Ecology, Climate and Empire: Colonialism and Global Environmental History, 1400–1940*, Cambridge: The White Horse Press, 1997.

12. T. Basset and D. Crummey (eds), *African Savannas, Global Narratives and Local Knowledge of Environmental Change*, London: James Currey and Heinemann, 2003.

13. R. Guha and M. Gadgil, *The Fissured Land: An Ecological History of India*, Oxford: Oxford University Press, 1992.

14. K. Jacoby, *Crimes against Nature: Squatters, Poachers, Thieves, and the Hidden History of American Conservation*, Berkeley and Los Angeles: University of California Press, 2014.

15. B. Cooke and U. Kothari, *Participation: The New Tyranny?* New York: Zed Books, 2001.

16. E. Said, *Culture and Imperialism*, London: Vintage, 1993.

17. G.C. Spivak, *A Critique of Postcolonial Reason: Towards a History of the Vanishing Present*, Cambridge, MA: Harvard University Press, 1999.

18. P. Gilroy, *Postcolonial Melancholia*, New York: Columbia University Press, 2004.

19. B. Latour, *Science in Action: How to Follow Scientists and Engineers through Society*, Cambridge, MA: Harvard University Press, 1987.

20. F. Cooper, *Colonialism in Question: Theory, Knowledge, History*, Berkeley, Los Angeles and London: University of California Press, 2005.

Chapter 1 Deconstructing Our Beliefs, (Re)thinking Nature

1. Author interview with Samson, Debark, 4 January 2019.
2. UNESCO, 'Decisions Adopted during the 41st Session of the World Heritage Committee', Kraków (Poland), 2017', p. 27 (whc. unesco.org/archive/2017/whc17-41com-18-en.pdf)
3. Ibid.
4. D. Brockington and J. Igoe, 'Eviction for Conservation: A Global Overview', *Conservation and Society*, 4-3, 2006, pp. 424–70.
5. C. Geisler, 'A New Kind of Trouble: Evictions in Eden', *International Social Science Journal*, 55, 2003, pp. 69–78.
6. L. Semal, *Bestiaire disparu. Histoire de la dernière grande extinction*. Toulouse: Éditions Plume de carotte, 2013.
7. L. Semal, *Face à l'effondrement. Militer à l'ombre des catastrophes*, Paris: PUF, 2019, p. 11.
8. Huffpost/AFP, 'Bolsonaro accuse à nouveau Macron de "colonialisme"', *Huffingtonpost*, 26 August 2019, https://www.huffing tonpost.fr/entry/bolsonaro-accuse-a-nouveau-macron-de-colo nialism_fr_5d63e6b4e4b02cc97c910dc2.
9. B. Akinro and J. Segun-Lean, 'Beyoncé and the Heart of Darkness', *Africa Is a Country*, https://africasacountry.com/2019/09/beyon ces-heart-of-darkness.
10. D. Leloup, 'Écofascisme: comment l'extrême droite en ligne s'est réappropriée les questions climatiques', *Le Monde*, 4 October 2019, https://www.lemonde.fr/pixels/article/2019/10/04/ecofas cisme-comment-l-extreme-droite-en-ligne-s-est-reappropriee-les-questions-climatiques_6014255_4408996.html.
11. W. Huismann, *Pandaleaks: The Dark Side of the WWF*, trans. Ellen Wagner, Bremen: Nordbook UG, 2014.
12. 'Exclusive: OECD Opens Investigations into WWF in World First', 5 January 2017, https://www.survivalinternational.org/news/11538.
13. F. Pigeaud, 'Le WWF accusé de "colonialisme vert" au Congo', *Mediapart*, 20 March 2019, https://mediapart.fr/journal/inter national/200319/le-wwf-accuse-de-colonialisme-vert-au-congo;

T. Warren and K.J.M. Baker, 'WWF Funds Guards Who Have Tortured and Killed People', *BuzzFeed News*, 4 March 2019, https://www.buzzfeednews.com/article/tomwarren/wwf-world-wide-fund-nature-parks-torture-death.

14. F. Walter, *Les Figures paysagères de la nation. Territoire et paysage en Europe (16ᵉ–20ᵉ siècle)*, Paris: Éditions EHESS, 2004, p. 178.

15. H. Mendras, *The Vanishing Peasant: Innovation and Change in French Agriculture*, Cambridge, MA: MIT Press, 1970.

16. Parc national des Cévennes, 'Rapport d'activité de l'établissement public chargé de la gestion du parc national et de la réserve de biosphère des Cévennes. 2001', Florac, 2002, p. 7.

17. E. O'Rourke, 'The Reintroduction and Reinterpretation of the Wild', *Journal of Agricultural and Environmental Ethics*, 13-1, 2000, pp. 145–65.

18. UNESCO, 'The Causses and the Cévennes, Mediterranean Agro-pastoral Cultural Landscape', https://whc.unesco.org/en/list/1153.

19. UNESCO, 'Simien National Park', https://whc.unesco.org/en/list/9/.

20. I. Grimwood, 'Ethiopia: Conservation of Nature and Natural Resources (November 1964–February 1965)', Paris, 1965, p. 4 (UNESCO, WS/0865.66).

Chapter 2 Turning Africa into Parkland (1850–1960)

1. *National Geographic*, special edition, *Les plus beaux parcs nationaux du monde*, 2017, pp. 12, 54 and 94.

2. R. Grove, *Green Imperialism: Colonial Expansion, Tropical Island Edens and the Origins of Environmentalism, 1600–1860*, Cambridge: Cambridge University Press, 1995.

3. J. Adams and T. McShane, *The Myth of Wild Africa: Conservation without Illusions*, Berkeley, Los Angeles and London: University of California Press, 1996, pp. xi–xix.

4. H. Stanley, *How I Found Livingstone: Travels, Adventures and Discoveries in Central Africa: Including an Account of Four*

Months' Residence with Dr Livingstone, London: Sampson Low, Marston, Low and Searle, 1872, pp. 423 and 455.

5. R. Neumann, 'Churchill and Roosevelt in Africa: Performing and Writing Landscapes of Race, Empire, and Nation', *Annals of the Association of American Geographers*, 103-6, 2013, p. 1380.

6. E. Said, *Orientalism: Western Conceptions of the Orient*, London: Penguin, 2006; F.-X. Fauvelle, *À la recherche du sauvage idéal*, Paris: Seuil, 2017.

7. R. Pankhurst and D. Johnson, 'The Great Drought and Famine of 1888–1892 in North-east Africa', in D. Johnson and D. Anderson (eds), *The Ecology of Survival: Case Studies from Northeast African History*, London: Lester Crook, 1988, pp. 47–72.

8. B. Gissibl, 'German Colonialism and the Beginnings of International Wildlife Preservation in Africa', *GHI Bulletin Supplement*, 3, 2006, pp. 121–43.

9. C. Ross, *Ecology and Power in the Age of Empire: Europe and the Transformation of the Tropical World*, Oxford: Oxford University Press, 2017, p. 274.

10. P. Anker, *Imperial Ecology: Environmental Order in the British Empire, 1895–1945*, Cambridge, MA: Harvard University Press, 2001.

11. D. Davis, *The Arid Lands: History, Power, Knowledge*, Cambridge, MA: MIT Press, 2016.

12. D. Davis, 'Desert "Wastes" of the Maghreb: Desertification Narratives in French Colonial Environmental History on North Africa', *Cultural Geographies*, 11-4, 2004, pp. 359–87.

13. Ibid.

14. J. MacKenzie, *The Empire of Nature: Hunting, Conservation and British Imperialism*, Manchester: Manchester University Press, 1988.

15. V. Pouillard, *Histoire des zoos par les animaux. Contrôle, impérialisme, conservation*, Seyssel: Champ Vallon, 2019, pp. 249–54.

16. R. Fitter and Sir P. Scott, *The Penitent Butchers: The Fauna Preservation Society, 1903–1978*, London: Collins, 1978.

17. 'Agreements Concluded at the International Conference for

the Protection of the Fauna and Flora of Africa', London, 1933, p. 21 (House of Commons paper Cmd. 4453, Session 1932/1933, v.XXXVIII.I).

18. E. Hemingway, *The Snows of Kilimanjaro*, London: Penguin, 2004, p. 23.

19. K. Blixen, *Out of Africa*, London: Penguin, 2001, p. 321.

20. W. Adams, 'Nature and the Colonial Mind', in W. Adams and M. Mulligan (eds), *Decolonizing Nature: Strategies for Conservation in a Post-Colonial Era*, London: Earthscan, 2003, pp. 29–33.

21. W. Beinart, 'Soil Erosion, Conservationism and Ideas about Development: A Southern African Exploration, 1900–1960', *Journal of Southern African Studies*, 11-1, 1984, pp. 52–83.

22. V. Pouillard, 'Conservation et captures animales au Congo belge (1908–1960). Vers une histoire de la matérialité des politiques de gestion de la faune', *Revue historique*, 679, 2016, pp. 577–604.

23. R. Gary, *The Roots of Heaven*, trans. Jonathan Griffin, Boston: Godine, 2018, pp. 107 and 122.

24. W. Beinart, 'The Lion Queen', *Environmental History*, 12-2, 2007, pp. 283–6.

25. Y. Kuwahara, 'Japanese Culture and Popular Consciousness: Disney's *The Lion King* vs Tezuka's *Jungle Emperor*', *Popular Culture*, 31-1, 1997, pp. 37–8.

26. G. Maddox, '"Degradation Narratives" and "Population Time Bombs": Myths and Realities about African Environments', in S. Dovers, R. Edgecombe and B. Guest (eds), *South Africa's Environmental History: Cases and Comparisons*, Athens, OH: Ohio University Press, 2003, pp. 250–8.

27. F. Cooper, *Decolonization and African Society: The Labor Question in French and British Africa*, Cambridge: Cambridge University Press, 1996.

28. R. Neumann, 'The Postwar Conservation Boom in British Colonial Africa', *Environmental History*, 7-1, 2002, pp. 22–47.

29. D. Prendergast and W. Adams, 'Colonial Wildlife Conservation and the Origins of the Society for the Preservation of the Wild Fauna of the Empire (1903–1914)', *Oryx*, 37-2, 2003, pp. 251–60.

30. M. Leach and R. Mearns (eds), *The Lie of the Land: Challenging Received Wisdom on the African Environment*, Oxford: James Currey, 1996.

31. I. Parker and S. Bleazard (eds), *An Impossible Dream: Some of Kenya's Last Colonial Wardens Recall the Game Department in the British Empire's Closing Years*, Kinloss: Librario, 2001, p. v.

Chapter 3 A Special Project for Africa (1960–1965)

1. L. Brown, *Ethiopian Episode*, London: Country Life Limited, 1965, pp. 66–7.

2. M. Everett, 'Obituary. Leslie Hilton Brown, OBE, BSc, PhD (1917–1980)', *British Birds*, 74-5, 1981, pp. 223–6.

3. J. Huxley, 'The Treasure House of Wildlife', *The Observer*, 13 November 1960, pp. 23–4.

4. IUCN, 'The International Union for the Conservation of Nature and Natural Resources. African Special Project, Stage 1', *Oryx*, 6-3, 1961, pp. 143–70.

5. J. McCormick, *The Global Environmental Movement*, Chichester: John Wiley, 1995, p. 46.

6. WWF, 'WWF's History', https://wwfint.awsassets.panda.org/downloads/morgesmanifesto.pdf.

7. J. Hillaby, 'African Special Project. Stage 2 – The Arusha Conference', *Oryx*, 6-4, 1962, p. 213.

8. UNESCO, 'Resolution Adopted by the General Conference of Unesco at Its 12th Session', Paris, 12 December 1963, p. 6 (UNESCO, 12 C/DR/64).

9. A. Gascon, 'La forêt perdue d'Éthiopie, un mythe contemporain', in M. Chastanet (ed.), *Plantes et paysages d'Afrique, une histoire à explorer*, Paris: Karthala & Centre de recherches africaines, 1998, pp. 383–409.

10. H.P. Huffnagel, 'Agriculture in Ethiopia', Rome: Food and Agriculture Organization, 1961, pp. 405–6.

11. W. Logan, *An Introduction to the Forests of Central and Southern Ethiopia*, Oxford: Oxford University Press, 1946, pp. 23–7.

12. F. von Breitenbach, 'National Forestry Development Planning:

A Feasibility and Priority Study on the Example of Ethiopia',
Ethiopian Forestry Review, 3, 1962, p. 43.

13. J. McCann, 'The Plow and the Forest: Narratives of Deforestation
in Ethiopia, 1840–1992', *Environmental History*, 2-2, 1997,
pp. 138–59.

14. J. McCann, *Green Land, Brown Land, Black Land: An
Environmental History of Africa, 1800–1990*, Oxford and
Portsmouth, NH: Heinemann & James Currey, 1999, pp. 128–34.

15. J. Huxley, A. Gille, T. Monod, L. Swift and E.B. Worthington, *The
Conservation of Nature and Natural Resources in Ethiopia*, Paris,
1964, pp. 3 and 23 (UNESCO, NS/NR/47).

16. UNESCO, 'UNESCO Sends Nature Conservation Mission to
Ethiopia', Press Release, 2061, 1964 (EWCA, FR/12).

17. W. Adams, *Against Extinction: The Story of Conservation*,
London: Earthscan, 2004, p. 141.

18. J. Schauer, '"We Hold it in Trust": Global Wildlife Conservation,
Africanization, and the End of Empire', *Journal of British Studies*,
57-53, 2018, p. 521.

19. I. Grimwood, 'Ethiopia. Conservation of Nature and Natural
Resources (November 1964–February 1965)', Paris, 1965, p. 4
(UNESCO, WS/0865.66).

20. S. Macekura, *Of Limits and Growth: The Rise of Global Sustainable
Development in the Twentieth Century*, Cambridge: Cambridge
University Press, 2015, p. 1.

21. *Oryx*, 8-1/2/3, 1965.

22. M. Callon, 'Sociologie de l'acteur réseau', in M. Akrich, M. Callon
and B. Latour, *Sociologie de la traduction. Textes fondateurs*,
Paris: Presses des Mines, 2006, pp. 267–76.

23. L. Brown, 'Ethiopia. Conservation of Nature and Natural
Resources (30 December 1964 to 1 April 1965)', Paris, 1965,
pp. 8, 12 and 13 (UNESCO, WS/0865.192).

24. Letter from L. Brown to N. Simon (IUCN, Morges), Karen
(Kenya), 26 December 1963, p. 1 (EWCA, JB/10).

Chapter 4 The Expert and the Emperor (1965–1970)

1. Letter from J. Blower to Major Gizaw, Addis Ababa, 3 July 1967 (EWCA, JB/4-5).
2. Letter from Major Gizaw to J. Blower, Addis Ababa, 4 July 1967 (EWCA, JB/4-5).
3. J. Hodge, 'British Colonial Expertise, Post-Colonial Careering and the Early History of International Development', *Journal of Modern European History*, 8-1, 2010, pp. 24–46.
4. Letter from J. Blower to His Imperial Majesty, Addis Ababa, October 1965, pp. 3–4 (EWCA, JB/4-5).
5. Ethiopian Tourism Organization, 'Big Game in Ethiopia', Addis Abba, 1968, pp. 3–4 (EWCA/O).
6. J. Blower, 'National Parks and Wildlife Conservation', Addis Ababa, 1967 (EWCA, JB/4-5).
7. J. Blower, 'Wildlife and Tourism in Ethiopia', Addis Ababa, 1968, p. 2 (EW CA, JB/4-5).
8. Letter from J. Blower to Major Gizaw, Addis Ababa, April 1966 (EWCA, JB/4-5).
9. Letter from J. Blower to Dr J. Morton Boyd (The Nature Conservancy, London), Addis Ababa, 15 July 1969 (EWCA, JB/1).
10. C. Ross, *Ecology and Power in the Age of Empire: Europe and the Transformation of the Tropical World*, Oxford: Oxford University Press, 2017, pp. 380–414.
11. Letter from J. Blower to General Mebratu, Addis Ababa, August 1969 (EWCA, JB/4-5).
12. Letter from J. Blower to Ato Abeba Retta, Addis Ababa, 4 April 1969 (EWCA, JB/6).
13. D. Turton, 'The Mursi and National Park Development in the Lower Omo Valley', in D. Anderson and R. Grove (eds), *Conservation in Africa: People, Policies and Practice*, Cambridge: Cambridge University Press, 1987, p. 169.
14. J. Abbink, 'Authority and Leadership in Surma Society (Ethiopia)', *Africa: Rivista trimestrale di studi e documentazione dell'Istituto italiano per l'Africa e l'Oriente*, 52–53, 1997, p. 325.

15. L. Brown, 'Ethiopia's Wildlife Conservation Program', *Biological Conservation*, 1, 1969, p. 332.
16. M. Foucault, *The Order of Things: An Archaeology of the Human Sciences*, London and New York: Routledge, 2002.
17. J. Blower, 'Wildlife Conservation Boards. Hunting Licences', Addis Ababa, 1966 (EWCA, JB/4-5).
18. Ministry of Agriculture, 'Wildlife Conservation Regulations Issued Pursuant to the Game Proclamation of 1944', Addis Ababa, 1968 (EWCA, JB/9).
19. Letter from J. Blower to Ato Abeba Retta, Addis Ababa, 4 April 1969 (EWCA, JB/6).
20. J. Blower, telegrams sent to twenty-two conservationists, Addis Ababa, June 1966 (EWCA, JB/9).
21. J. Blower, 'Draft of Report Prepared for Board', Addis Ababa, 25 May 1968 (EWCA, JB/4-5).
22. Major Gizaw, 'Budget', Addis Ababa, November 1967 (EWCA, JB/4-5).
23. Ibid.
24. Letter from J. Blower to Major Gizaw, Addis Ababa, 15 February 1967 (EWCA, JB/4-5).
25. J. Blower, 'Development of Roads and Tracks in National Parks: Outline Programme of Work', Addis Ababa, 15 May 1968 (EWCA, JB/8).
26. EWCA, 'A Summary of the External Assistance Requested and Received by the Wildlife Conservation Organization', Addis Ababa, December 1975 (EWCA, JB/10).
27. D. Maingueneau, 'Les Rapports des organisations internationales: un discours constituant?', *Nouveaux Cahiers de l'IUED*, 13, 2002, p. 130.
28. A. Kirk-Greene, 'Decolonization: The Ultimate Diaspora', *Journal of Contemporary History*, 36-31, 2001, pp. 133–51.
29. L. Brown, 'Wildlife Conservation', Addis Ababa, 1971, p. 4 (EWCA, box/file 'Life 1970/Education').
30. Letter from D. Paradis to His Excellency Ghermatchew Telke Hawariat, Addis Ababa, July 1966 (EWCA, JB/6).

31. Letter from J. Blower to Major Gizaw, Addis Ababa, February 1967 (EWCA, JB/6).
32. J. Blower and L. Brown, 'Declaration of Wildlife Policy', Addis Ababa, 1968 (EWCA, JB/6); EWCO, 'Comments of the Wildlife Conservation Organization', Addis Ababa, 1972 (EWCA, JB/9).
33. Imperial Ethiopian Government, 'Order No. 65. Wildlife Conservation Order', *Negarit Gazeta*, 30-4, 5 November 1970, pp. 30–3.
34. J. Fairhead and M. Leach, *Misreading the African Landscape*, Cambridge: Cambridge University Press, 1996, p. 253.
35. UNESCO, 'UNESCO Sends Nature Conservation Mission to Ethiopia', Press Release, 2061, 1964 (EWCA, FR/12).
36. Haile Selassie, 'Preface', *Walia*, 1, 1969, p. 1.
37. L. Brown, 'Conservation of Nature and Natural Resources: Ethiopia – (Mission), 30 December 1964 to 1 April 1965. Report', Paris: UNESCO, 1965 (UNESCO, WS/0865.192/AVS).
38. EWCO, 'Comments of the Wildlife Conservation Organization', Addis Ababa, 1972 (EWCA, JB/9).
39. R. Neumann, *Imposing Wilderness: Struggles over Livelihood and Nature Preservation in Africa*, Berkeley and Los Angeles: University of California Press, 1998, pp. 144–5.
40. B. Gissibl, 'National Parks as Cosmopolitics', *RCC Perspectives*, 1, 2014, pp. 47–52.
41. Letter from J. Blower to His Excellency the vice-prime minister, Addis Ababa, 13 September 1965 (EWCA, JB/4-5).
42. Major Gizaw, 'Budget', Addis Ababa, December 1966 (EWCA, JB/4-5).
43. EWCO, 'Wildlife in Ethiopia. A Vanishing National Heritage and the Need to Conserve It', Addis Ababa, 1967, p. 6 (EWCA, O).
44. Ethiopian Imperial Government, 'Hunting Licence Regulations, Rules and Procedures', Addis Ababa, 1 September 1972 (EWCA).
45. Letter from Mebratu Fisseha to Dr Vollmar (WWF), Addis Ababa, 5 August 1969 (EWCA, JB/11).
46. Turton, 'The Mursi and National Park Development in the Lower Omo Valley'.

47. J. Blower, 'Proposals for the Development of the Simien Mountains National Park', Addis Ababa, April 1968 (EWCA, JB/11).
48. Letter from J. Blower to Major Gizaw, Addis Ababa, 22 February 1969 (EWCA, JB/1).
49. Letter from Major Gizaw to J. Blower, Addis Ababa, 25 March 1969 (EWCA, JB/1).
50. Letter from J. Blower to Major Gizaw, Addis Ababa, April 1966 (EWCA, JB/4-5).
51. Letter from J. Blower to Major Gizaw, Addis Ababa, May 1968 (EWCA, JB/5-5).
52. The Ethiopian language does not follow a rule such as family name/first name. The first name comes first, then the name of the father, followed by that of the grandfather. In general the first name is used.
53. Girma Tayachew, 'The Simien Wild Fauna under the Protection of the Government of Haile Selassie: From Endangered Prey to National Symbol (1941–1969)', *Annales d'Éthiopie*, 31, 2018, pp. 65–80.
54. Letter from C. Nicol to J. Blower, Gondar, 30 May 1969 (EWCA, JB/11).
55. Ethiopian Imperial Government, 'Order No. 59. Simien National Park Order', *Negarit Gazeta*, 29-4, 31 October 1969, pp. 6–8.
56. W. Beinart, 'Conservation Ideologies in Africa. Introduction', in D. Anderson and R. Grove (eds), *Conservation in Africa: People, Policies and Practice*, Cambridge: Cambridge University Press, 1987, p. 169.

Chapter 5 Violence Below the Surface of Nature (1970–1978)

1. M. Mok, 'The Losing Fight for Game Parks', *Life*, 69-19, 27 November 1970, p. 57.
2. F. Locher, 'Cold War Pastures: Garrett Hardin and the Tragedy of the Commons', *Revue d'histoire moderne et contemporaine*, 60-1, 2013, pp. 7–36.

3. N. Peluso and M. Watts, 'Violent Environments', in N. Peluso and M. Watts (eds), *Violent Environments*, Ithaca, NY, and London: Cornell University Press, 2001, pp. 3–38.

4. M. Foucault, *'Society Must be Defended': Lectures at the Collège de France 1975–1976* (eds M. Bertani and A. Fontana; trans. D. Macey), London: Penguin, 2004, p. 29.

5. Letter from C. Nicol to Abeba Retta, Gondar, 8 July 1969 (EWCA, JB/1).

6. Letter from J. Blower to General Mebratu, Addis Ababa, 16 July 1969 (EWCA, JB/11).

7. Letter from J. Bromley to General Mebratu, Addis Ababa, 13 February 1970 (EWCA, JB/4).

8. WWF, *Yearbook, 1971–1972*, Morges, 1972, p. 81.

9. G. Sprecher, 'Introduction', *Geographica Bernensia Simen Mountains – Ethiopia*, 1978, p. 7.

10. C. Nicol, 'A Census of the People of Geech and the Livestock at Geech', Addis Ababa, 27 May 1969 (EWCA, JB/1); P. Stähli, 'Changes in Settlement and Land Use in Simen, Ethiopia, Especially from 1954 to 1975', *Geographica Bernensia Simen Mountains – Ethiopia*, 1978, p. 58.

11. H. Hurni, 'Simien Mountains National Park, Provision of a Game Warden', in WWF, *Yearbook, 1975–1976*, Morges, 1976, p. 62.

12. Girma Tayachew, 'The Simien Wild Fauna under the Protection of the Government of Haile Selassie: From Endangered Prey to National Symbol (1941–1969)', *Annales d'Éthiopie*, 31, 2018, pp. 65–80.

13. Ethiopian Tourism Commission, *Endemic Mammals of Ethiopia*, Addis Ababa, 1982.

14. Imperial Ethiopian Government, 'Order no. 65. Wildlife Conservation Order', *Negarit Gazeta*, 30-4, 5 November 1970, pp. 30–3.

15. Imperial Ethiopian Government, 'Regulations Issued Pursuant to the Game Proclamation of 1944 and the Wildlife Conservation Order of 1970', *Negarit Gazeta*, 31-7, 19 January 1972, pp. 35–52.

16. H. Hurni, 'Soil Erosion Forms in the Simien Mountains – Ethiopia

(with Map 1:25 000)', *Geographica Bernensia Simen Mountains – Ethiopia*, 1978, p. 94.

17. T. Shatto, 'Report from: Safaris International', Chicago, October 1965 (EWCA, JB/6).

18. J. Mellon. 'The Abyssinian Ibex, or Walia. A Shoot on the Heights and Abysses of Semien', in J. Mellon (ed.), *The African Hunter*, Safari Press, 1975, pp. 189–96.

19. J. Blower, 'Draft of Report prepared for Board. Summary of Progress', Addis Ababa, May 1969 (EWCA, JB/4-5).

20. P. Stähli and M. Zurbuchen, 'Two Topographic Maps 1:25,000 of Simien, Ethiopia', *Geographica Bernensia Simen Mountains – Ethiopia*, 1978, p. 21.

21. L. Brown, 'Ethiopia. Progress Report on the Imperial Ethiopian Government's Three Years Wildlife Development Plan', Nairobi, UNESCO & RCSTA, 7 June 1968, p. 13 (EWCA, O).

22. Letter from J. Dandoi (United States Peace Corps Ethiopia, Addis Ababa) to T. Demmet, Addis Ababa, 12 June 1969 (EWCA, JB/8).

23. L. Brown, 'Wildlife Conservation', Addis Ababa, 1971, p. 4 (EWCA, O).

24. Ethiopian Tourism Commission, 'Simien National Park Information Sheet', Addis Ababa, 1976 (EWCA).

25. EWCO, 'National Parks and Wildlife Legislation in Ethiopia', Addis Ababa, 1976, p. 9 (EWCA, FR).

26. Ethiopian Tourism Commission, 'Simien National Park Information Sheet', Addis Ababa, 1976 (EWCA).

27. Stähli, 'Changes in Settlement and Land Use in Simen, Ethiopia', p. 57.

28. Mok, 'The Losing Fight for Game Parks', p. 57.

29. P. Stracey, 'A Brief Note on a Visit to Simien National Park', Addis Ababa, 11 February 1972, p. 3 (EWCA, JB/11).

30. M. Bolton, 'S.F. Request for a National Parks and Conservation Planning Project', Addis Ababa, 13 April 1970 (EWCA, JB/10).

31. Letter from P. Stracey to General Mebratu, Addis Ababa, 22 February 1972 (EWCA, JB/11).

32. EWCA, 'A Summary of the External Assistance Requested and

Received by the Wildlife Conservation Organisation from May 1972 to December 1975', Addis Ababa, 1976 (EWCA, JB/10).

33. EWCO, 'Annual Report', Addis Ababa, 1978.
34. WWF, *Yearbook 1971–1972*, p. 81.
35. WWF, *Yearbook 1975–1976*, p. 59.
36. Sprecher, 'Introduction', p. 7.
37. UNESCO, 'Convention Concerning the Protection of the World Cultural and Natural Heritage', Paris, 1972, p. 1.
38. Ethiopia Tikdem, 'A Draft Proclamation to Provide for the Conservation and Management of Wildlife', Addis Ababa, 1975, p. 18 (EWCA, JB/9).
39. Ethiopia Tikdem, 'Endangered Species of Wildlife Conservation Commemorative Coins Regulations', *Negarit Gazeta*, 37-13, 21 June 1978, p. 76 (EWCA).
40. UNESCO, 'Second General Assembly of States Parties to the Convention Concerning the Protection of the World Cultural and Natural Heritage', Washington, DC, 1978, p. 7 (UNESCO, CC-78/CONF.010/10 Rev).
41. EWCO, 'Annual Report'.
42. Letter from Stracey to Mebratu, 22 February 1972.
43. EWCO, 'Fourth Five Year Plan', Addis Ababa, 1973, p. 19.
44. J. Stephenson, 'Memorandum on the Draft Proclamation to Provide for the Conservation and Management of Wildlife', Addis Ababa, 20 November 1975, p. 1 (EWCA, JB/9).
45. Lealem Berhanu, 'Development and Utilisation of Wildlife in Coordination with Livestock and Range Management', Addis Ababa, 1976, p. 1 (EWCA, FR/1).

Chapter 6 The Sustainable Development Trap (1978–1996)

1. Ermias Bekele, 'A Description of the Conservation Status and Future Outlooks of Ethiopia's Semien Mountains, Bale Mountains, and Abijata Shalla Lakes National Parks. UNESCO's World Heritage Mission to Ethiopia. April 24', Addis Ababa, 1982, p. 12 (EWCA).

2. T. Luke, 'Environmentality as Green Governmentality', in E. Darier (ed.), *Discourses of the Environment*, Oxford: Blackwell Publishers, 1999, pp. 121–51.

3. F. Giraut, S. Guyot and M. Houssay-Holzschuch, 'La nature, les territoires et le politique en Afrique du Sud', *Annales: Histoire, Sciences Sociales*, 60-4, 2005, pp. 695–717.

4. R. Neumann, 'Political Ecology of Wildlife Conservation in the Mt Meru Area of Northeast Tanzania', *Land Degradation & Rehabilitation*, 3, 1992, pp. 85–98.

5. P. Katembo Vikanza, *Aires protégées, espaces disputés et développement au nord-est de la R.D. Congo*, Louvain la Neuve: Presses universitaires de Louvain, 2011, p. 138.

6. Bahru Zewde, *A History of Modern Ethiopia, 1855–1991*, London: James Currey, 2002, pp. 235–56.

7. C. Rossetti, 'Draft Report on a Mission to Semien (1–15 Feb. 1981) on Behalf of UNESCO in Connection with World Heritage Fund', Addis Ababa, 1981, p. 5 (EWCA).

8. Ermias Bekele, 'A Description of the Conservation Status and Future Outlooks of Ethiopia's Semien Mountains', p. 13.

9. Ethiopia Tikdem, 'Management Planning Considerations for the Simien Mountain National Park. A Report on a Unesco/World Heritage Workshop. March 22, 1983', Addis Ababa, 1983, pp. 6–9 (EWCA).

10. J.-N. Bach, 'Centre, périphérie, conflit et formation de l'État depuis Ménélik II: les crises *de* et *dans* l'État éthiopien (XIX – XX siècle)', Ph.D. thesis in political science, University of Bordeaux 4 Montesquieu, 2011, pp. 394–403.

11. Letter from Tilahun Bezabeh to Kebele 04 of Debre Febres Seber, 1985 (SMNPO, PO).

12. EWCO, 'A Development Plan for Wildlife Conservation in Ethiopia', Addis Ababa, 1985, p. 23 (EWCA).

13. EWCO and UNESCO, 'Management Plan. Simen Mountains National Park and Surrounding Rural Area', 1986, pp. 11, 20, 26, 59, 49 and 62 (EWCA).

14. T. Lekan, *Our Gigantic Zoo: A German Quest to Save the*

Serengeti, Oxford: Oxford University Press, 2020, p. 256. See also T. Lekan, '*Serengeti Shall Not Die*: Bernhard Grzimek, Wildlife Film, and the Making of a Tourist Landscape in Africa', *German History*, 29-2, 2011, pp. 224–64.

15. EWCO and UNESCO, 'Management Plan', p. 84.

16. Letter from J. Hillman to D. Shackelton (IUCN), Addis Ababa, 18 October 1989 (EWCA, IUCN).

17. J. Hillman, 'Simien Mountains National Park: Visit Report', Addis Ababa, 1991, p. 7 (SMNPO).

18. Letter from Meheret Meteku to the Office of the Simien National Park in Debark, May 1991 (SMNPO); Ethiopian Wildlife and Natural History Society, 'Important Bird Areas of Ethiopia. A First Inventory', Addis Ababa, 1996, p. 2 (EWCA).

19. Hillman, 'Simien Mountains National Park: Visit Report', p. 4.

20. M. Honey, *Ecotourism and Sustainable Development: Who Owns Paradise?* Washington, DC, and Covelo, CA: Island Press, 1999.

21. IUCN, UNEP and WWF, 'World Conservation Strategy. Living Resource Conservation for Sustainable Development', Gland (Switzerland), 1980, pp. 2–4.

22. World Commission on Environment and Development, *Our Common Future*, Oxford: Oxford University Press, 1987.

23. G.H. Brundtland, 'How to Secure Our Common Future', *Scientific American*, September 1989, p. 190.

24. United Nations, 'Convention on Biological Diversity', Rio de Janeiro, 5 June 1992, p. 3.

25. A. Agrawal and C. Gibson, 'Enchantment and Disenchantment: The Role of Community in Natural Resource Management', *World Development*, 27-4, 1999, pp. 629–49.

26. G. Rist, *The History of Development: From Western Origins to Global Faith*, London: Zed Books, 2019.

27. S. Tomasini, 'Unpacking the Red List: Use (and Misuse?) of Expertise, Knowledge, and Power', *Conservation & Society*, 16-4, 2018, pp. 505–17.

28. J. Adams and T. McShane, 'The Scientists Take Over', in *The Myth of Wild Africa: Conservation without Illusions*, Berkeley,

Los Angeles and London: University of California Press, 1996, pp. 85–108.

29. D. Chatty and M. Colchester (eds), *Conservation and Mobile Indigenous Peoples: Displacement, Forced Settlement and Sustainable Development*, New York and Oxford: Berghahn Books, 2002.

30. D. Brockington, *Fortress Conservation: The Preservation of the Mkomazi Game Reserve, Tanzania*, Oxford: James Currey in association with International African Institute, 2002.

31. W. Beinart and K. McKeown, 'Wildlife Media and Representations of Africa, 1950s to the 1970s', *Environmental History*, 14-3, 2009, pp. 429–52.

32. C. Lutz and J. Collins, *Reading National Geographic*, Chicago: University of Chicago Press, 1993.

33. W. Adams, 'Nature and the Colonial Mind', in W. Adams and M. Mulligan (eds), *Decolonizing Nature: Strategies for Conservation in a Post-Colonial Era*, London and Stirling, VA: Earthscan, 2003, pp. 16–17.

34. A. Hoben, 'Paradigms and Politics: The Cultural Construction of Environmental Policy in Ethiopia', *World Development*, 23-6, 1995, pp. 1007–21.

35. Teshome Ashine, 'Wildlife Conservation', in EWCO and IUCN, *National Conservation Strategy*, vol. 3, Addis Ababa, 1990, pp. 8–9 (EWCA).

36. Hillman, 'Simien Mountains National Park: Visit Report', p. 10.

37. D. Crabtree, 'Proposal for the Rehabilitation of the Simien Mountains National Park, Ethiopia', Gondar, 1993, p. 8 (EWCA).

38. Farm Africa, 'A Reconnaissance of Simen Mountains National Park and Buffer Zone, 23rd March–4th April 1994', Addis Ababa, 1994, p. 19 (EWCA).

39. A. Agrawal and C. Gibson (eds), *Communities and the Environment: Ethnicity, Gender, and the State in Community-Based Conservation*, New Brunswick, NJ: Rutgers University Press, 2001.

40. EWCO and WWF, 'Establishment of a Trust Fund for Ethiopia's Protected Areas', Addis Ababa, 1996, p. 9 (EWCA).

41. EWCO and Farm Africa, 'Workshop on the Simien Mountains National Park Management. Gondar, February 15–17 1995. Proceedings', Addis Ababa, 1995, pp. 24–5 (EWCA).

42. EWCO and Farm Africa, 'Participatory Wildlife Management Workshop. Proceedings 16–18 May 1995', Addis Ababa, 1995, p. 76 (EWCA).

43. H. Hurni and B. Nievergelt, 'Technical Mission to Ethiopia on Simien Mountains National Park and World Heritage Site, 2–9 November 1996. Consultant's Report Including Agreed Minutes of Bahir Dar Workshop', Bahir Dar, 1996, p. 24 (EWCA).

44. UNESCO, '20th Session of the World Heritage Committee. Report', Mérida (Mexico), 1996, pp. 28–9 (UNESCO, WHC-96/ CONF.201/21).

45. B. Müller, 'Comment rendre le monde gouvernable sans le gouverner: les organisations internationales analysées par les anthropologues', *Critique internationale*, 54-1, 2012, pp. 9–18; P.B. Larsen, 'The Politics of Technicality: Guidance Culture in Environmental Governance and the International Sphere', in B. Müller (ed.), *The Gloss of Harmony: The Politics of Policy-Making in Multilateral Organisations*, London: Pluto Press, 2013, pp. 80–102.

Chapter 7 The Fiction of the Community Approach (1996–2009)

1. E. Edroma and K.H. Smith, 'Monitoring Mission Report to Simen Mountains National Park and World Heritage Site, Ethiopia', Addis Ababa, 2001, p. 17 (EWCA).

2. L. Brown, 'A Report on the Wild Life Situation in the Semien Mountains of North Ethiopia', Addis Ababa, 1963, p. 3 (EWCA).

3. Edroma and Smith, 'Monitoring Mission Report to Simen', p. 14 (EWCA).

4. G. Debonnet, L. Melamari and B. Bomhard, 'Reactive Monitoring Mission to Simien Mountains National Park, Ethiopia', Addis Ababa, 2006, p. 13 (EWCA).
5. J. Tilman, 'IUCN. Reactive Monitoring Mission to Simien National Park, Ethiopia', Addis Ababa, 2017, p. 20 (EWCA).
6. P. Stähli, 'Changes in Settlement and Land Use in Simen, Ethiopia, Especially from 1954 to 1975', *Geographica Bernensia Simen Mountains – Ethiopia*, 1978, p. 58.
7. B. Nievergelt, T. Good and R. Güttinger, 'A Survey of the Flora and Fauna of the Simen Mountains National Park, Ethiopia', *Walia: Journal of the Ethiopian Wildlife and Natural History Society*, 1998, p. 92.
8. D. Crummey, 'Deforestation in Wällo: Process or Illusion?', *Journal of Ethiopian Studies*, 31-1, 1998, pp. 1–41.
9. J. McCann, *Green Land, Brown Land, Black Land: An Environmental History of Africa, 1800–1990*, Portsmouth, NH, and Oxford: Heinemann & James Currey, 1999.
10. M. Leach and J. Fairhead, 'Challenging Neo-Malthusian Deforestation Analysis in West Africa's Dynamic Forest Landscapes', *Population and Development Review*, 26-1, 2000, pp. 17–43.
11. A. Gore, *Earth in the Balance: Ecology and the Human Spirit*, Boston: Houghton Mifflin, 1992, p. 107; *An Inconvenient Truth: The Planetary Emergence of Global Warming and What We Can Do about It*, Emmaus, PA: Rodale Books, 2006, p. 148. (James McCann was the first historian to point out Gore's appropriation of the myth of the lost forests in Ethiopia.)
12. T. Luke, 'The Politics of True Convenience or Inconvenient Truth: Struggles over How to Sustain Capitalism, Democracy, and Ecology in the 21st century', *Environment and Planning A*, 40, 2008, pp. 1811–24.
13. E. Garland, 'The Elephant in the Room: Confronting the Colonial Character of Wildlife Conservation in Africa', *African Studies Review*, 51-3, 2008, pp. 51–73.
14. PADPA, 'Status Report of the World Natural Heritage Site,

Simien Mountains National Park (Ethiopia)', Bahir Dar, 2008, p. 10 (PADPA).

15. A. Pankhurst and F. Piguet (eds), *Moving People in Ethiopia: Development, Displacement and the State*, Melton, Suffolk: James Currey, 2009.

16. Democratic Federal Republic of Ethiopia, 'The Conservation Strategy of Ethiopia. Executive Summary', Addis Ababa, 1997, p. 20 (EWCA).

17. M. Keiner, 'Simen Mountains National Park Management Plan', Landeck (Austria), 2000, p. 77 (PADPA).

18. PADPA, 'Development of Alternative Livelihoods for the Population of the Simen Mountains National Park, Ethiopia', Bahir Dar, 2006, p. 14 (PADPA).

19. PADPA, 'Simen Mountains National Park Integrated Development Project, Project 1722-00. Terminal Report', Debark, 2007 (SMNPO).

20. Yeshaw Tenaw, 'Report', 2003, Debark (SMNPO).

21. PADPA, 'Simen Mountains National Park Integrated Development Project. Quarter Report, April 1 to June 31', Debark, 2005 (SMNPO).

22. PADPA, 'Grazing Pressure Reduction Strategy for Simen Mountains National Park. Draft Report', Bahir Dar, 2007 (PADPA).

23. Negussie Tsegaye, 'Report', 2006, Debark (SMNPO).

24. G. Blanc and M. Bridonneau, 'Politiques patrimoniales dans le *Simien Mountains National Park*. Quels enjeux pour quel territoire? Rapport d'étude de terrain', Addis Ababa (Centre français des études éthiopiennes), 2007, p. 22.

25. D. Hulme and M. Murphree, 'Communities, Wildlife and the "New Conservation" in Africa', *Journal of International Development*, 11, 1999, p. 279.

26. B. Büscher, 'Payments for Ecosystem Services as Neoliberal Conservation: (Reinterpreting) Evidence from the Maloti-Drakensberg, South Africa', *Conservation and Society*, 10-1, 2012, pp. 29–41.

27. F. Verdeaux and B. Roussel, 'Y a-t-il un autochtone dans l'avion? Des ethnies locales à l'autochtonie globale en passant par la gestion durable de la biodiversité', *Autrepart*, 38-2, 2006, pp. 15–37.
28. E. Morin, *La Méthode*, vol. 5: *L'humanité de l'humanité. L'identité humaine*, Paris: Seuil, 2001, pp. 221–2.
29. Nievergelt et al., 'A Survey on the Flora and Fauna', p. 92.
30. H. Hurni, *Decentralised Development in Remote Areas of the Simien Mountains, Ethiopia*, Bern: Centre for Development and Environment, 2005, p. vii.
31. PADPA, 'Simen Mountains National Park Integrated Development Project. Project Plan, October 2005–March 2007', Debark, 2005, p. 51 (SMNPO); Asfaw Menasha, 'Yearly Report', Debark, 2009 (SMNPO); noted by the author in April 2007, May 2009, April 2010 and November 2012.
32. Fante Teshagre, 'Report. Gich', Debark, 2008 (SMNPO).
33. Berhanu Gebre Mohammed, 'Report. Agedemya', Debark, 2005 (SMNPO).
34. Desire Gabreze, 'Report. Sankaber', Debark, 2008 (SMNPO).
35. Ali Reta, 'Report', Debark, 2009 (SMNPO).
36. G. Cazes, *Les Nouvelles colonies de vacances? Le tourisme international à la conquête du Tiers-Monde*, Paris: L'Harmattan, 1999.
37. K.M. Woodhouse, *The Ecocentrists: A History of Radical Environmentalism*, New York: Columbia University Press, 2018, pp. 183–234.
38. PADPA, 'Simien Mountains National Park Management Plan', Addis Ababa, 2006, pp. 25–35 (EWCA).
39. EWCA, 'State of Conservation Report on Simien Mountains National Park, World Natural Heritage Site (Ethiopia)', Addis Ababa, 2014, pp. 10–11 (EWCA).
40. H. Hurni and B. Nievergelt, 'Technical Mission to Ethiopia on Simien Mountains National Park and World Heritage Site, 2–9 November 1996. Consultants' Report Including Agreed Minutes of Bahir Dar Workshop', Bahir Dar, 1996, p. 15 (EWCA).
41. PADPA, 'Simien Mountains National Park Integrated

Development Project, Project 1722-00', Bahir Dar, 2007, p. 8 (PADPA).

42. PADPA, 'Status Report of the World Natural Heritage Site, Simien Mountains National Park', p. 7.
43. Tilman, 'IUCN. Reactive Monitoring Mission to Simien National Park, Ethiopia', p. 5.
44. Bekalu Ademasu, 'Report', Debark, 2007 (SMNPO, WD).
45. Negussie Gebre, 'Report. Lemalimo', Debark, 2008 (SMNPO).
46. Letter from Berhanu Gebre to the courts in Debark, Debark, 2002 (SMNPO, JF); Mola Anderge, 'Report. Adamarz', Debark, 2009 (SMNPO).
47. Berhanu Gebre, 'Report', Debark, 2002; Zekele Tegabe, 'Report', Debark, 2005; Abebe Mengesha, 'Report', 2006, Debark; Yisak Yiman, 'Report. Arkwasiye', Debark (SMNPO).
48. J. Wolfensohn, P. Seligmann and M. El-Ashry, 'Winning the War on Biodiversity Conservation', *New Perspectives Quarterly*, 17-4, 2000, pp. 38–9.
49. R. Neumann, 'Moral and Discursive Geographies in the War for Biodiversity in Africa', *Political Geography*, 23, 2004, pp. 813–37.
50. Wolde Gabriel, 'Report. Adi Arkay', Debark, 2002 (SMNPO).
51. Berhanu Gebre, 'Report. Dirni', Debark, 2002 (SMNPO).
52. Berara Tadles, 'Report. Sawre', Debark, 2008 (SMNPO).
53. Debonnet et al., 'Reactive Monitoring Mission to Simien Mountains National Park, Ethiopia', p. 11.
54. EWCA, 'State of Conservation Report of the World Heritage Site, Simien Mountains National Park (Ethiopia)', Addis Ababa, 2015, p. 7 (EWCA).
55. PADPA, 'Simien Mountains National Park General Management Plan 2009–2019', Bahir Dar, 2009, p. 46 (PADPA).
56. K.I. MacDonald, 'Global Hunting Grounds: Power, Scale and Ecology in the Negotiation of Conservation', *Cultural Geographies*, 12, 2005, p. 282.
57. Author interview with Samuel, Debark, 13 April 2010.

Chapter 8 The Roots of Injustice (2009–2019)

1. Author interview with Philippos, Ambaras, 3 January 2019.
2. Tiru Berihun Tessema, M. Jungmeier and M. Huber, 'The Relocation of the Village of Arkwasiye in the Simien Mountains National Park in Ethiopia: An Intervention towards Sustainable Development?', *eco.mont*, 4-2, 2012, pp. 13–20.
3. Eyobe Mesfin, Derje Amene and Ashenafi Taffess, 'Alternative Livelihood Options for Gich Local Community. A Perspective on Sustainable Tourism Development: The Case of Newly Resettle Site of Debark/Semin Mountain National Park, Ethiopia', *International Journal of Hospitality & Tourism Systems*, 10-2, 2017, pp. 14–21.
4. P. Howard and A. Makarigakis, 'UNESCO and IUCN Reactive Monitoring Mission to Simien National Park (Ethiopia)', Addis Ababa, 2009 (EWCA).
5. UNESCO, 'State of Conservation of the Properties Inscribed on the List of World Heritage in Danger', Brasilia (Brazil), 2010, pp. 16–21 (UNESCO, WHC-10/34, COM/7A.Add).
6. EWCA, 'State of Conservation Report on Simien Mountains National Park, World Natural Heritage Site (Ethiopia)', Addis Ababa, 2014, pp. 10–11 (EWCA).
7. EWCA, 'State of Conservation Report of the World Natural Heritage Site, Simien Mountains National Park (Ethiopia)', Addis Ababa, 2017, pp. 4–13 (EWCA).
8. M. Cernea, 'For a New Economics of Resettlement: A Sociological Critique of the Compensation Principle', *International Social Science Journal*, 55-175, 2004, pp. 37–45.
9. P.B. Larsen and D. Brockington (eds), *The Anthropology of Conservation NGOs: Rethinking the Boundaries*, London: Palgrave Macmillan, 2018.
10. The interviews carried out in Amharic would not have been accurately transcribed without the help of Mehdi Labzaé, doctor of political sciences.
11. EWCA, 'State of Conservation Report of the World Natural Heritage Site, Simien Mountains National Park (Ethiopia)', p. 5;

UNESCO, 'Decisions Adopted during the 41st Session of the World Heritage Committee', Kraków (Poland), 2017 (UNESCO, WHC/17/41.COM/18).

12. Translator's note: in Amharic the word used is '*tch'na*'.

13. É. Balibar, *Justice and Inequality: A Political Dilemma? Pascal, Plato, Marx*, Kolkata: Mahanirban Calcutta Research Group, 2007.

14. EWCA, 'State Party Report on the Conservation of the World Natural Heritage Site, Simien Mountains National Park (Ethiopia)', Addis Ababa, 2018, p. 12 (EWCA).

15. J. Tilman, 'IUCN. Reactive Monitoring Mission to Simien National Park, Ethiopia', Addis Ababa, 2017, p. 20 (EWCA); UNESCO, 'State of Conservation of the Properties Inscribed on the World Heritage List', Kraków, 2017, p. 29 (UNESCO, WHC/17/41.COM/7A.Add.2).

16. UNESCO, 'State of Conservation of the Properties Inscribed on the World Heritage List', Manama (Bahrain), 2018, p. 199 (UNESCO, WHC/18/42.COM/7B).

17. Democratic Federal Republic of Ethiopia, 'Proclamation No. 541. Ethiopian Wildlife Conservation Authority Proclamation', *Negarit Gazeta*, 14-8, 2008 (EWCA).

Conclusion

1. UNESCO, 'World Heritage List', https://whc.unesco.org/en/list/.

2. Cited by R. Neumann, *Imposing Wilderness: Struggles over Livelihood and Nature Preservation in Africa*, Berkeley, Los Angeles and London: University of California Press, 1998, p. 34.

3. J. Verschuren, *Ma Vie. Sauver la nature*, Deurle: Éditions de la Dyle, 2001, p. 19.

4. UNESCO, 'Convention for the Safeguarding of the Intangible Cultural Heritage', Paris, 2003 (UNESCO, CL/3696).

5. D. Quammen, 'Saving Africa's Eden', *National Geographic*, September 2003, pp. 50–73.

6. M. Schwartz, 'Real-Life "Tarzan" Lee White Is on a Mission to

Protect Gabon's Forest Elephants', 24 June 2016, http://www.mi chaelwschwartz.com/articles.html.

7. IUCN, 'The International Union for the Conservation of Nature and Natural Resources. African Special Project, Stage 1', *Oryx*, 6-3, 1961, p. 143.

8. Observed by the author, April 2019.

Afterword: Looking Ahead

1. Cited by Le Point Afrique, 'Parcs naturels africains: vous avez dit "colonialisme vert"?', *Le Point*, 20 September 2020, https://www. lepoint.fr/afrique/parcs-naturels-africains-vous-avez-dit-colo nialisme-vert-20-09-2020-2392745_3826.php.

2. E. Ottone Ramirez, 'En Afrique, "faire de la protection de la nature un grand dessein colonial n'est pas sérieux"', *Le Monde*, 1 November 2020, https://www.lemonde.fr/afrique/article/2020/ 11/01/en-afrique-faire-de-la-protection-de-la-nature-un-grand-dessein-colonial-n-est-pas-serieux_6058115_3212.html.

Index

220 Index

Index